Herbert Puchta & Jeff Stranks
G. Gerngross C. Holzmann P. Lewis-Jones

MORE! 3

Student's Book

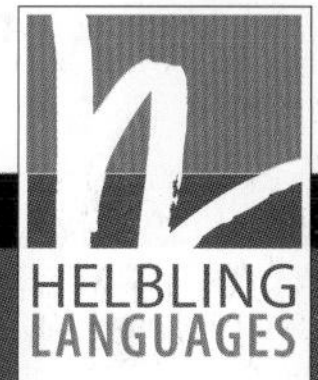

	Grammar	Language Focus and Vocabulary	Skills	MORE!
UNIT 1 I've left my camera at home	• present perfect • irregular past participles • *how long …?/ for/ since*	• words for objects **Sounds right** /h/	• ask where people have been • give advice • ask about how long • ask about dreams • read a questionnaire • listen to a conversation • write about your best friend **A Song 4 U** *You've got a friend*	Learn **MORE** through English **That nasty flu!** **Biology**
UNIT 2 Steven Spielberg Superstar	• present perfect *yet/already* • present perfect with *just* • present perfect v past simple	• words for types of film	• say what you have done • say what films you like/ don't like • read book summaries • listen to the story of a film • write a film review	**Check your progress** Units 1 and 2 Learn **MORE** about culture **The European Union** Read **MORE** for pleasure **Casino Royale**
UNIT 3 We're going to use it today	• *will* • *going to* • reflexive pronouns	• words for geographical features **Sounds right** stress in compound nouns	• say what you are going to do • talk about preferences • talk about plans/offers • read a short story • listen to a description of an adventure camp • talk about sports activities • write about an adventure camp	Learn **MORE** through English **Glaciers** **Geography**
UNIT 4 Superstitions!	• prepositions • common verbs plus prepositions • phrasal verbs	• words for star signs	• talk about superstitions • talk about star signs • find out about people • listen, read and understand a play • listen and summarise a play • write a review of a story	**Check your progress** Units 3 and 4 Learn **MORE** about culture **Modern books and writers** Read **MORE** for pleasure **Two wishes**
UNIT 5 It's easy, isn't it?	• relative pronouns *who/which/that* • question tags	• words for places **Sounds right** intonation in question tags	• ask for information at the cinema • read a historical text • listen to teenagers talking • write a short letter **A Song 4 U** *Waterloo Sunset*	Learn **MORE** through English **The history of London** **History**
UNIT 6 Young people today	• present simple passive • *make* and *let*	• words for jobs **Sounds right** /i/ vs. /iː/	• talk about ambition • say where things are done • say what people let you do • read and understand a magazine article • listen to the story of a USA immigrant • speak about what your parents make and let you do • write about your family	**Check your progress** Units 5 and 6 Learn **MORE** about culture **English around the world** Read **MORE** for pleasure **Burundi boy**

Unit	Grammar	Language Focus and Vocabulary	Skills	MORE!
UNIT 7 I didn't use to like them	• *used to* • *so do I / neither do I*	• words for music	• talk about what you used to do • agree and disagree • read and match texts and photos • listen to a TV programme • speak about performers on a show • write a summary about a pop star or band **A Song 4 U** *Weekend*	Learn **MORE** through English **Musical instruments** **Music**
UNIT 8 Natural disasters	• *too/ not … enough* • past passive	• words for catastrophes **Sounds right** 'r' sound	• express sympathy • explain things in simpler words • talk about when people were born • read and understand a story • listen to the story of an earthquake • speak about things to take to a desert island • write about someone who survived an earthquake	**Check your progress** Units 7 and 8 Learn **MORE** about culture **Manga!** Read **MORE** for pleasure **How to survive earthquakes**
UNIT 9 If I had the money …	• second conditional • *If I were you …* • indefinite pronouns *everyone, someone, no one, anyone*	• words for computers	• give advice • talk about people • talk about what you would do • ask about how long • read about dilemmas • listen to teenagers talking about dilemmas • complete a questionnaire • write a questionnaire **A Song 4 U** *If I were you*	Learn **MORE** through English **Number challenges** **Maths**
UNIT 10 Into the wilderness	• make deductions • causative *have* • infinitives of purpose	• words for holidays **Sounds right** Question intonation	• give reasons • talk about holiday plans • make deductions • read emails about a trip • listen to an email • write a summary	**Check your progress** Units 9 and 10 Learn **MORE** about culture **Gap year abroad** Read **MORE** for pleasure **The leopard that lost its spots**
UNIT 11 He told us not to worry	• reported speech • *want/ask/tell* someone to do something	• words for the environment	• say what you want people to do • read and write about ecology • listen to people talking about their heroes/heroines • talk about your heroes • write a leaflet **A Song 4 U** *We shall overcome*	Learn **MORE** through English **Energy and how to save it** **Science**
UNIT 12 California	• reported speech 2	• words for physical appearance **Sounds right** Word stress	• justify options • identify a person • read a description of Los Angeles • talk about Los Angeles • write about California **A Song 4 U** *California Dreaming*	**Check your progress** Units 11 and 12 Learn **MORE** about culture **What a waste!** Read **MORE** for pleasure **The sound of California**

Word list

UNIT 1 I've left my camera at home.

In this unit

You learn
- present perfect
- irregular past participles
- *how long …?/ for/ since*
- words for objects

and then you can
- ask about where people have been
- give advice
- ask about how long
- ask about dreams

1 Read and listen to the dialogue.

Claire Hi Oliver! I haven't seen you for ages. How are you?
Oliver Great thanks Claire. How were your holidays?
Claire Brilliant. I had a really good time. We went to Edinburgh for a week.
Oliver Lucky you! I've always wanted to go there, but I've never had the chance. My parents don't like travelling much.
Claire Pity. It's a great place.
Oliver Yeah. Lots of people have told me that. Well, maybe I'll go there one day.
Claire Of course you will! Oh, by the way, Oliver – have you got Tom Atkinson's phone number? I want to get in touch with him, and I've lost his number.
Oliver I guess you haven't heard. Tom doesn't live here any more. His family's moved to Manchester. He's been there since last month.
Claire Really? That's a shame. I wanted to show him my photos of Edinburgh. He's really into photography, and I took some good shots.
Oliver Well, I've got his email, maybe you could send the photos to him. Listen Claire, I'm really hungry. Do you fancy getting something to eat?
Claire Yes – I'm starving! I haven't eaten anything since breakfast. Let's try the new hamburger place on King Street. Have you ever been there?
Oliver No. So that's two places I've never been to! How long has it been open?
Claire About three months, I think. I've heard it's good.
Oliver OK, let's go. You can show me your photos while we eat.
Claire Well, no, actually! I've left my camera at home!

2 **Write Claire, Oliver or Tom in each sentence.**

1 .... has been to Edinburgh.
2 .... has never been to Edinburgh.
3 .... hasn't heard about Tom.
4 .... has moved to Manchester.
5 .... likes photography a lot.
6 .... has lost a telephone number.
7 .... hasn't eaten since breakfast.
8 .... has never been to the hamburger place.

Get talking Asking where people have been

3 **3** **Listen and repeat.**

Boy 1 Have you ever been to France?
Girl 2 No, I haven't. Have you?
Boy 1 Yes, I have.

Girl 1 Hi, Tom. I haven't seen you since Sunday. Where have you been?
Boy 1 I've been at my grandmother's. For five days!

4 **Ask and answer questions. Use the words on the left and the pictures below.**

England
Spain
USA
France
Germany

A Have you ever been to England?
B Yes, I have. / No, I haven't.

A I haven't seen you since yesterday / Monday / this morning. Where have you been?
B I've been ill.

Language Focus

Vocabulary Objects

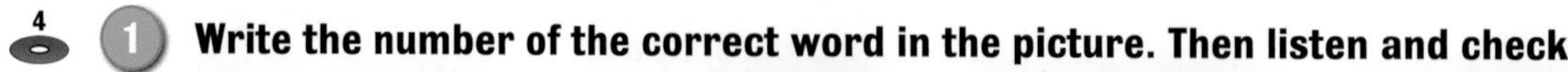

4 **1** **Write the number of the correct word in the picture. Then listen and check.**

1 sunglasses
2 mobile phone
3 CD player
4 MP3 player
5 digital camera
6 palmtop
7 headphones
8 games console

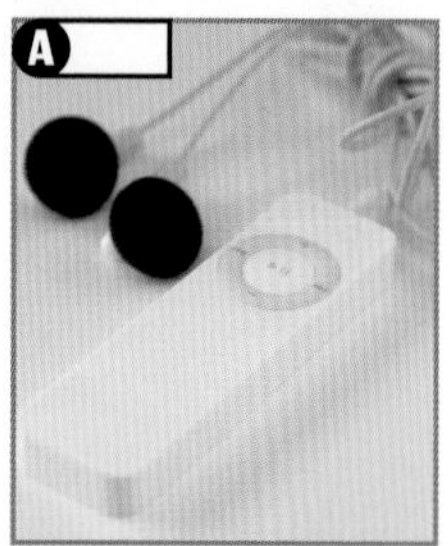

Get talking Giving advice

2 **Work in pairs. Look at the pictures. Give advice using the expressions below.**

A Why don't you …? / You should …

B OK! Good idea! / OK! I will!

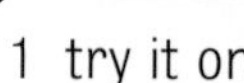

1 try it on

2 take a picture

3 use these

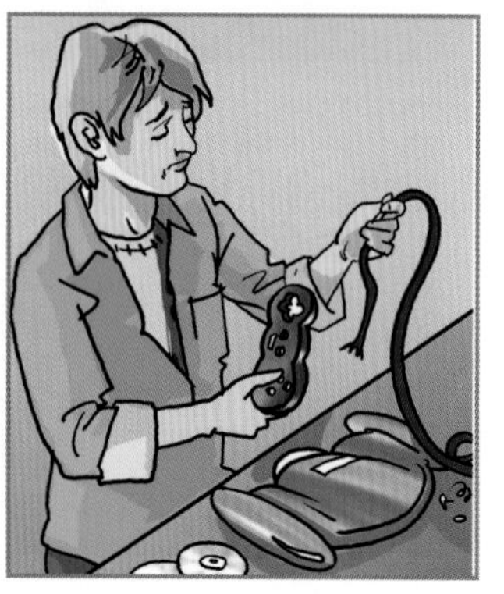

4 take it back

5 copy them

6 switch it off

Grammar

Present perfect

1 Complete the sentences with the verbs. Check with the dialogue on page 4.

heard
left
wanted
moved

I've always [1] .... to go there. (= and I still want to go)
You **haven't** [2] .... (= so you don't know about it)
His family**'s** [3] .... to Manchester. (= so he doesn't live here any more)
I've [4]...................... my camera at home! (= so I can't show you the photographs)

We use the Present Perfect to talk about actions that happened or began in the past (it doesn't matter exactly ***when***) and are still relevant ***now.*** (Read the examples in brackets above.)
We often use the Present Perfect with ***ever*** (in questions) and ***never*** (in negative statements).
Have you **ever been** there? **I've never had** the chance.

2 Complete the tables with *has / hasn't / have* or *haven't*.

Positive
I / You / We / They have finished.
He / She / It [1] .... finished.

Negative
I / You / We / They [2].......... finished.
He / She / It hasn't finished.

Questions
[3].......... I / you / we / they finished?
[4].......... he / she / it finished?

Short answers
Yes, I / you / we / they [5].......... / No, I / you / we / they [6]..........
Yes, he / she / it [7].......... / No, he / she / it [8]..........

3 Complete the sentences with the correct form of the Present perfect.

1 He has ...*worked*....... hard today. (work)
2 My bike is dirty – I .... it. (not wash)
3 .... the match ....? (finish)
4 We .... always .... here. (live)
5 My brother .... never .... a laptop. (want)

Irregular past participles

gone take run seen had said buy make

4 Complete the table with the appropriate verb.

be – been	[3]................ – bought	catch – caught	come – come
do – done	eat – eaten	find – found	go – [7]................
have – [1]................	know – known	[5]................ – made	[8]................ – run
say – [2]................	see – [4]................	[6]................ – taken	think – thought

5 Complete the sentences.

1 I'm hungry – I *haven't eaten* anything today. (not eat)
2 He's here now. He's .... out. (be)
3 They aren't here – they .... to the shopping centre. (go)
4 I .... never .... that film. Is it any good? (see)
5 .... you ever .... of learning Russian? (think)

How long......? for / since

6 **Complete with one word in each space. Check with the dialogue on page 4.**

I haven't seen you [1] .... ages.
He's been in Manchester [2] .... last month.
How [3] .... has it been open?

Use ***for*** to talk about a period of time: **for two hours / for three days / for a year.**
Use ***since*** to say the exact time when an action or situation began: **since 2005 / since 10 o'clock / since last Friday.**

Use ***how long........?*** to ask a question about the duration of an action or situation.

7 **Complete with *for* or *since*.**

1 I've had my MP3 player .....since..... Christmas.
2 I've had my palm top .... six months.
3 My father's worked in that office .... two years.
4 They've lived in that flat .... 2004.

8 **Write questions using *How long...?* for the answers in Exercise 7.**

Get talking Asking about how long

5 **9** **Put the dialogue into the correct order. Listen and check.**

☐	**Roland**	About a month. It's super.
☐	**Interviewer**	So, do you use it a lot?
1	**Interviewer**	Hi Roland. Tell me, what's your favourite possession?
☐	**Roland**	Sure, I play games on it and take pictures, and even videos. I've taken a video of my English lesson. Do you want to see it?
☐	**Interviewer**	How long have you had it?
☐	**Roland**	Hmmm, my mobile phone, I suppose.
☐	**Interviewer**	Maybe another time, thanks!

Get talking Asking about dreams

10 **Match the sentence halves. Then practise them with a partner.**

1 I've wanted to go to Argentina since I was a student,
2 I've always wanted to climb a really high mountain,
3 I've always wanted to learn the saxophone,
4 I've always wanted to meet a famous person
5 I've always wanted to sing in a band,
6 I've always wanted to be a writer

a but I've never climbed a mountain higher than 3,000 metres!
b and I've practised hard, but no band wants an opera singer.
c but I never have.
d because I saw a film about tango-dancing there.
e and now I write instructions for laptops.
f but I've never found the time to take lessons.

Skills

Reading

1 **Do the questionnaire.**

What kind of friend are you?

1 Your best friend hasn't phoned you for two weeks. What do you do?

a ☐ You look for a new friend.
b ☐ You sulk for some time.
c ☐ You call your friend and try to meet him / her.

2 You have a problem. Your friend asks you what it is. What do you do?

a ☐ You say that you don't want to talk about your problem.
b ☐ You share your problem with your friend.
c ☐ You get angry and tell your friend to mind his / her own business.

3 You've got a new hair cut, but your friend says that you look awful. What do you do?

a ☐ You aren't happy, but you know that good friends are honest.
b ☐ You never talk to your friend again.
c ☐ You tell your friend that you don't like his / her hair cut either.

4 Your best friend has been ill for three weeks. Last week, you found another friend. Today your best friend is back at school. What do you do?

a ☐ You tell your best friend about your new friend.
b ☐ You don't talk to your new friend any more.
c ☐ You tell your best friend that you haven't got time to meet him / her any more.

5 You haven't been to the cinema since last Christmas. There's a great film on tonight. You want to go, but your friend wants to go to a party. What do you do?

a ☐ Your friend goes to the party, you go to see the film, and you are still friends.
b ☐ You don't want to be friends with someone who doesn't like what you like.
c ☐ You say that you don't really want to see the film and go along to the party.

Check your result!

Points:

1 a: 1	**b:** 2	**c:** 3
2 a: 2	**b:** 3	**c:** 1
3 a: 3	**b:** 1	**c:** 2
4 a: 3	**b:** 2	**c:** 1
5 a: 2	**b:** 1	**c:** 3

0 – 5 points:
It's probably not easy to be friends with you. Try to be a bit more understanding! Then you'll make good friends.

5 – 10 points:
Lots of people would like to be friends with you. You haven't found your best friend yet. Take it easy – you soon will.

10 – 15 points:
You're an excellent friend, and friendship is really important for you. Other people love being with you. Congratulations!

A Song 4 U You've got a friend

2 **Look at the words of the song. Put the words in the correct places. Listen and check.**

Close
clouds
door
friend
hurt
loud
need
nights

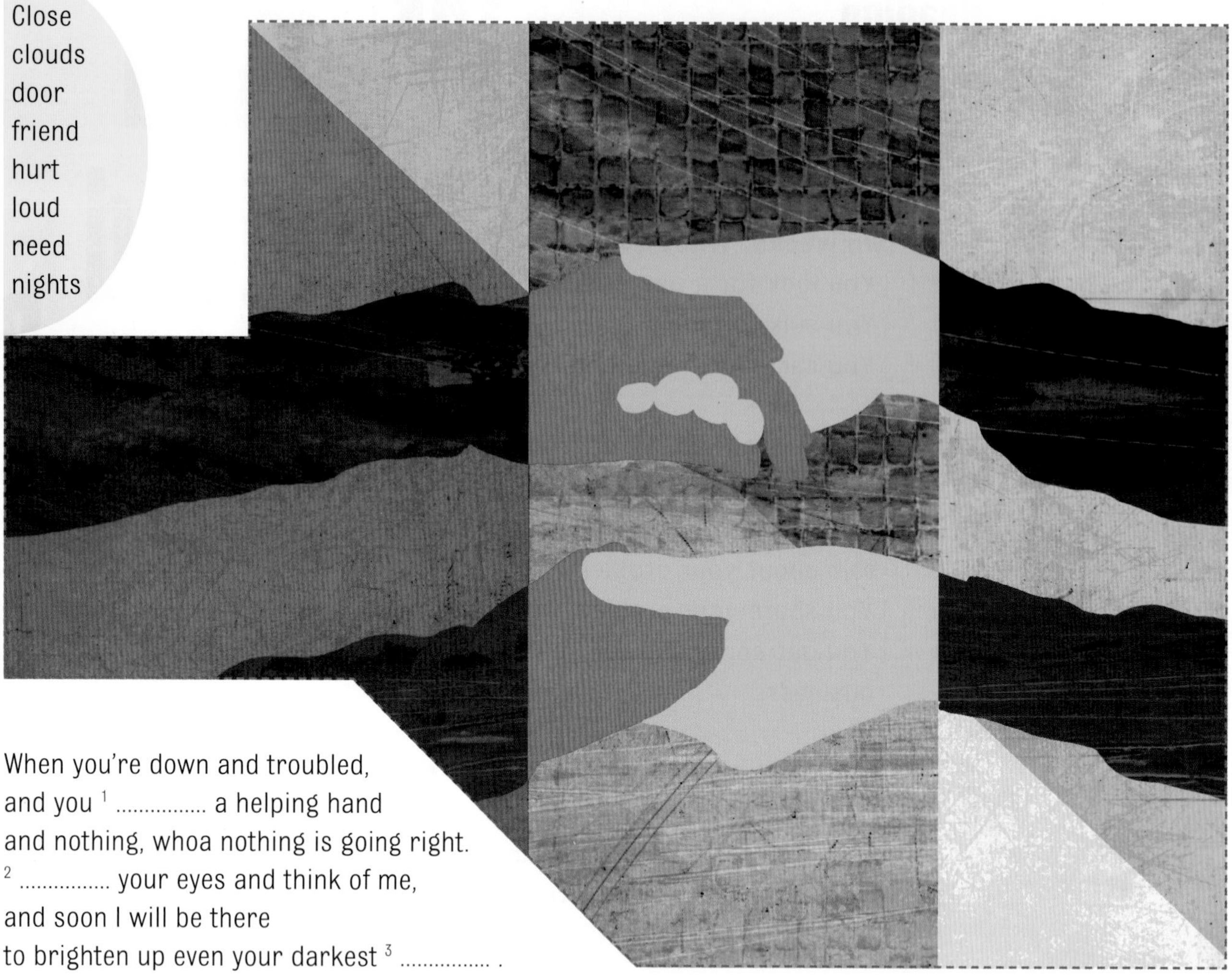

When you're down and troubled,
and you [1] .... a helping hand
and nothing, whoa nothing is going right.
[2] .... your eyes and think of me,
and soon I will be there
to brighten up even your darkest [3] ....

You just call out my name, and you know wherever I am,
I'll come running, oh yeah baby, to see you again.
Winter, spring, summer or fall,
all you got to do is call,
and I'll be there, yeah, yeah, yeah.
You've got a friend.

If the sky above you should turn dark and full of [4] .... ,
and that old north wind should begin to blow.
Keep your head together and call my name out [5] .... ,
and soon I will be knocking upon your [6] ....

Chorus

Hey ain't it good to know that you've got a [7] .... ,
when people can be so cold?
They'll [8] .... you and desert you,
Well they'll take your soul if you let them.
Oh yeah, but don't you let them.

Chorus

Sounds right /h/

3 Listen and repeat.

1 Have you heard about Harry?
2 He's here and he isn't happy.
3 I haven't had a holiday for a year.
4 They had a horrible holiday in Harlow!

Listening and speaking

4 Complete the sentences with the words on the left. Then listen and check. Talk about your best friend.

lies
listens
lends
hear
keeps

1 My best friend always .... me things when I need them. (Sue, 14)
2 Good friends don't just say what you want to .... (James, 14)
3 A good friend .... to your problems. (Les, 13)
4 A good friend always .... a secret for you. (Ken, 13)
5 A good friend never .... to you. (Sharon, 13)

Writing for your Portfolio

5 Read about Joanna's best friend.

My best friend is Nadia. I've known her for six years. We've been friends since our first day at school together. She's really kind and she always helps me if I've got a problem. She's really good at maths, too – she has helped me with homework lots of times! We do a lot of things together – we go to the cinema and we play games. She often stays at my house, and I often stay at hers. We've never had a big argument, only little ones. I think we'll always be friends.

6 Write a short text about your best friend.

That nasty flu!

Key words

temperature	virus	immune system
pain	inhabitants	catastrophic consequences
miserable	sneeze	a flu shot
illness	cough	medication

1 **Headache, high body temperature and pain all over the body – when you have influenza, or flu as it is usually called, you feel really miserable. Find out why this illness can be quite dangerous – and what you can do about it.**

It was November 1918 in Alaska and a ship had just arrived at a nearby harbour. The 80 people in the tiny village of Teller heard about an illness that the people on the ship had brought with them. But they did not care – they did not often get visitors and they were very happy to see people from outside. They organised a big party for the people on the ship.

The people from Teller did not know that their visitors were carrying a deadly virus. Only a week later most of the people from Teller fell ill. Another week later 72 out of the 80 inhabitants were dead!

Teller is only one example. In the winter of 1918/19, the illness – called 'Spanish' flu – killed more than 50 million people all over the world. Flu comes every year, and most people have had it once. Usually flu is not dangerous, but sometimes it is. In fact, in the twentieth century there were two more 'pandemics'. A pandemic is a global outbreak of an illness with catastrophic consequences. In 1957 the 'Asian' flu and in 1968 the 'Hong Kong' flu killed lots of people. In recent years there has been fear of 'bird flu' after humans were infected by a virus carried by birds.

INFLUENZA

In many countries doctors recommend getting a flu shot before the flu season starts. This is what you can do when you already have the flu:

- Stay in bed
- Drink lots of liquid like water and fruit juice
- Take medicine for fever, aches and pains
- Cover each cough and sneeze with a handkerchief
- Keep warm

We hope you're flu-free this year, but if you do get flu, now you know what to do!

2 How does flu spread?

Influenza spreads through viruses. You get them when you breathe in little drops that spray from an infected person when they sneeze, cough, or even laugh. You can also catch flu if the drops get on your hands and you touch your mouth or nose. Influenza viruses are very good at entering a body. They have lots of spikes. With these spikes they stick to cells and travel through the body.

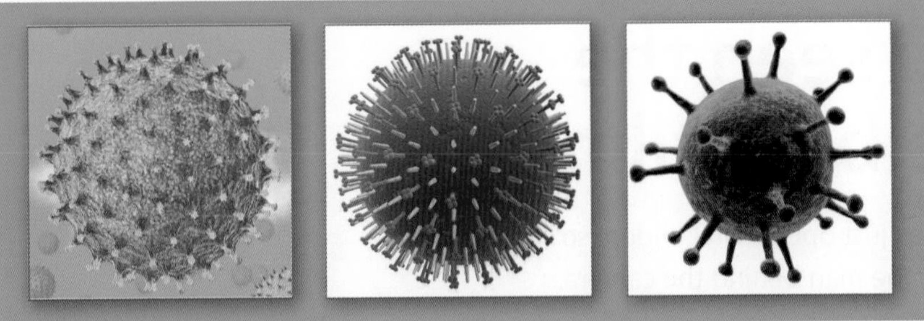

Viruses

When the body's immune system notices the viruses, it raises body temperature. When body temperature is higher, the virus cannot multiply so easily.

Normally, with the help of medication, it takes the immune system about a week to win the fight against flu. So why can influenza be so dangerous? Because small children and old people do not have a very strong immune system. But also because the influenza virus often changes. Scientists often have to develop new medication.

Mini-project illnesses

3 Use a dictionary. Find the names of these illnesses in your language.

tuberculosis chicken pox food poisoning malaria

Choose one of the illnesses. Search the internet or check in the library to answer the following questions:

1 What causes the illness? A virus? Something else?
2 Who normally gets the illness?
3 Is it a dangerous illness?
4 What can you do when you get it?
5 Have you ever had this illness yourself?

Flu is an illness that often occurs during the cold months. It spreads through viruses, and it is especially dangerous for older people and small children. If you have flu, you have to stay in bed for about a week. You should drink a lot, and take medication.
I always get a flu shot before the cold months start. I think it helps.

UNIT 2 Steven Spielberg Superstar!

Read the magazine article about Steven Spielberg.

Film and theatre **NEWS & REVIEWS**

Have you seen the new Spielberg film yet?

The new ***Spielberg*** film has just opened in London, so we thought we'd take a closer look at the man behind the camera.
Laura Davis reports:

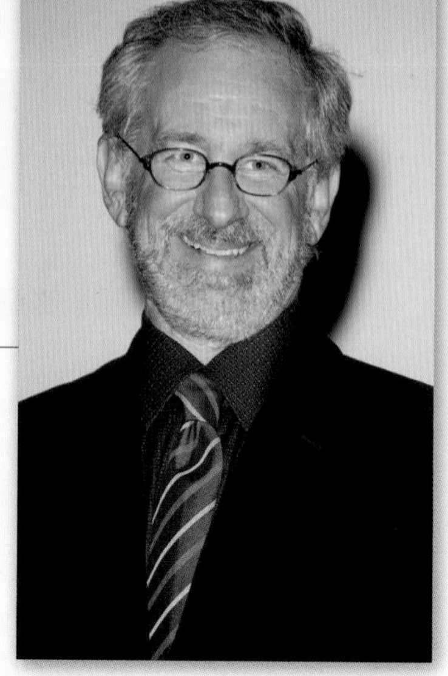

People were afraid to go into the sea after *Jaws*. They wanted to be archaeologists after *Raiders of the Lost Ark*. They thought dinosaurs were real after *Jurassic Park*. They cried when they watched *E.T.* and *Schindler's List*. They were shocked by the realities of war in *Saving Private Ryan*. They laughed at *The Terminal* and *Catch Me If You Can*. And they were amazed by the special effects in *War of the Worlds*. And all this because of one man – Hollywood's best-known film director, producer and writer: Steven Allan Spielberg.

Spielberg was born in Cincinnati, Ohio on 18th December 1946. Today he and his films are famous all over the world. He has already won several Oscars and Golden Globes. He has directed more than twenty-five films, and produced more than fifty. He hasn't starred in any of his films yet, but don't be too surprised if you see him on the screen one day.

Has Steven always been so successful? In a word – yes. He made his first amateur film, an 8-minute Western called *The Last Gun*, when he was twelve. And he has always been an excellent businessman. When he showed his home movies to other children, he sold tickets, and his sister Annie sold popcorn.

Did you know?

The **producer** controls the preparation of a film and gets the money for production together.
The **director** is the person who tells the actors how to act in front of the camera.

In this unit

You learn

- present perfect *yet/already*
- present perfect with *just*
- present perfect v past simple
- words for types of film

and then you can

- say what you have done
- say what films you like/ don't like
- talk about films

2 **Circle T (True) or F (False) for the sentences below.**

1 He has won various prizes for his films. T / F
2 Spielberg only directs films. T / F
3 When he was 12, he made his first film. T / F
4 He sold popcorn to the kids who came to see his film. T / F

Get talking Saying what you have done

9 **3** **Listen and repeat.**

A Has Dave seen the new Orlando Bloom film yet?
B Yes, he saw it last night.

A Has Dave done his maths homework yet?
B No, he hasn't.

4 **Work with a partner. Study the table for a minute. A: ask B four questions. Then change over.**

A Has Dave read the new Dan Brown book yet?
B Yes, he has. He finished it two hours ago.

finish / new Dan Brown book	✓ (two hours ago)
write / an email to Steve	✗
do / history homework	✗
buy / *Top Car* magazine	✓ (this morning)
listen to / new *Editors* CD	✗
finish / the model airplane	✓ (on Monday)
see / new Jennifer Lopez film	✓ (last night)
study / for his English test	✓ (last week)

5 **Think of some recent popular films, books, computer games, CDs or magazines and ask your partner if they have seen, read, or heard them.**

A Have you seen the new James Bond film?
B Yes, I saw it on Sunday. It was great!

Language Focus

Vocabulary Types of film

10

1 **Read the article about some of Spielberg's most famous films. Write the correct type of film under each picture. Then listen and check.**

1

2

3

4

5

6

It is difficult to choose a favourite Spielberg film – there are so many and he never makes a bad one. Some love his **war** films like *Saving Private Ryan*. Other people go for his **science fiction** films such as *Close Encounters* and *E.T.*

Maybe you prefer his **adventure** films like the *Indiana Jones* series. Or the **epic** *Schindler's List*. As a producer he was responsible for **animated cartoons** such as *Shrek* and even **horror** films like *Poltergeist*.

Spielberg has always surprised his audiences with the types of film he makes and he will surprise us again in the future with something different. After all, his first film was a **western**.

7

Get talking Saying what films you like / don't like

11

2 **Listen and repeat.**

A What do you think of adventure films?
B I think they're exciting.

A What do you think of epic films?
B I don't really like them. They're always too long.

3 **Ask and answer questions about films with a partner. Use these words and phrases to help you.**

boring   always the same   funny   creative   violent   scary

A What do you think of ...

B I think they're ...

Grammar

Present perfect + *yet / already*

1 **Look back at the text on page 14 and complete the examples.**

He has [1].................... won several Oscars and Golden Globes.
He hasn't starred in any of his films [2]....................
Have you seen the new Spielberg film [3]....................?

You use [4].................... at the end of questions and negative sentences.
You use [5].................... in positive sentences.

2 **Match the sentences to the correct pictures.**

A 

B 

C 

D 

1 She hasn't found the answer yet.
2 The mechanic hasn't fixed her car yet.
3 They haven't phoned her yet.
4 The breakdown service hasn't arrived yet.

3 **Complete the sentences with *yet* or *already*.**

1 Have you seen the new Spiderman film ....?
2 He's .... directed 4 films and he's only 30.
3 We haven't bought our tickets ....
4 I've .... seen this film twice.
5 They've .... finished filming the new Superman film.
6 Has the new James Bond film opened ....?

4 **Use these words to write sentences. Use *just*, *yet* or *already*.**

1 Dana / get / new Keane CD.
Dana's already got the new Keane CD.
2 Nathan / finish reading / the new Philip Pullman book.
3 Phillip Pullman / not finish / new book.
4 Julia / start / a diet.
5 John / see / the new Jude Law film.
6 Olivia / not see / Lion King.

Present perfect with *just*

5 **Put the words in order to make the example sentence. Check with the text on page 14.**

new in has just London. The opened film Spielberg

We use *just* in positive sentences to say that something has happened a short while ago.

6 **Write sentences in the Present perfect.**

1 already / film / begin ...*The film has already begun.*...
2 already / I / be to the cinema twice this week ....
3 just / they / ask for you ....
4 just / she / hear some fantastic news ....

Present perfect v past simple

7 **Complete the sentences with the Present perfect or Past simple. Check with the text on page 14.**

He [1]...................... (direct) more than twenty-five films.
He [2]...................... (make) his first film when he was 12.
He [3]...................... (always be) an excellent businessman.
When he [4]...................... (show) his home movies to other children he [5]...................... (sell) tickets.

We use the Present perfect to talk about an undefined past time. When we talk about a specific time we use the Past simple.

8 **Choose the correct form of the verb. Complete the sentences.**

1 I *have found* the money. Here it is! (found / have found)
2 I .... to London for the first time two years ago. (went / have gone)
3 Carmen .... a wonderful cake. Would you like to try it? (made / has made)
4 My parents .... me a new video game last week. (gave / have given)
5 In 2003, my brother .... to New York. (moved / has moved)
6 Claire and I .... friends. We really like each other now. (have become / became)

Get talking Talking about films

12 **9** **Listen to the interviews and answer the questions.**

1 How many times has Monica seen *Jaws*?
2 How many times has Monica read the book?
3 Why didn't she go swimming when she first saw the film?
4 Has Dan seen *Jurassic Park*?
5 When did he see *Schindler's List*?
6 Where has Emma seen the Indiana Jones films?

10 **Work in pairs. Talk about these films. Use the words below to help you.**

A Have you seen any good films recently?
B I saw…
A What did you like about it?

The actors were
- brilliant.
- great.
- good-looking.
- funny.

The story was
- exciting.
- unusual.
- funny.
- real.

The special effects were
- wonderful.
- cool.
- excellent.

Skills

Reading

1 **Steven Spielberg has turned many short stories and novels into films. Here are some of the books he used. Match the book covers and the descriptions**

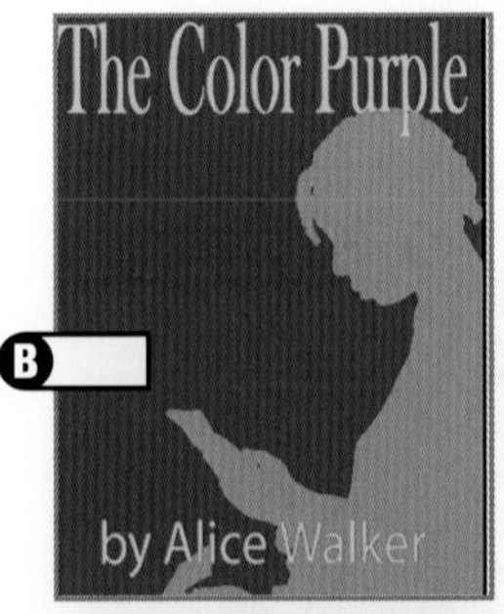

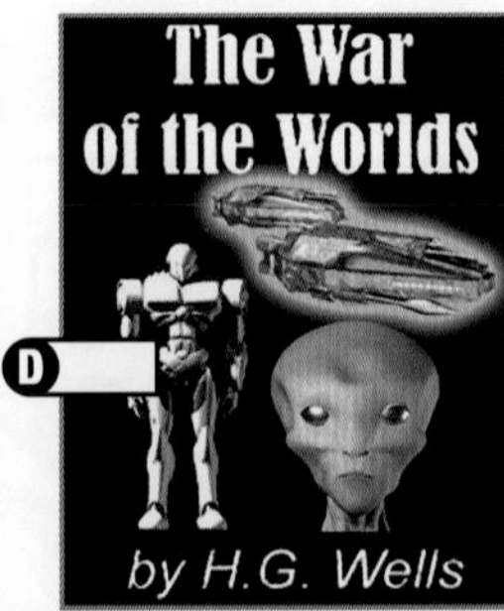

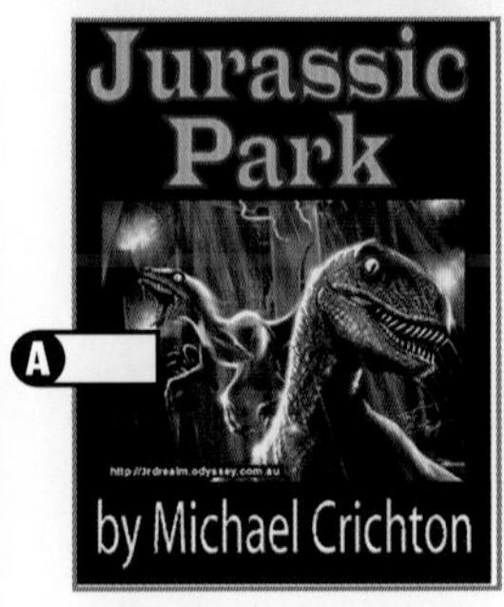

1 This is the story of a young black woman called Celie, who has to live with a man she doesn't like. However, her woman friends help her as much as the can.
2 One day a shark attacks a young lady swimming at night – and then the terror begins. A small town in America faces its biggest nightmare. Don't pick the book up before midnight!
3 A scientist's dream turns into a nightmare when things go very wrong in his theme park on an island in the Pacific.
4 The story of a man who helped thousands of Jews to escape the Nazi terror during the Second World War.
5 The adventures of three children in Neverland – a classic children's story, filmed by Spielberg under the title Hook.
6 Set in the future, this story is about a police chief. His officers can predict who will commit a crime. One day they predict that he will kill a man he doesn't even know.
7 Martians come to earth and build huge killing machines. Can the people from Earth fight back? A classic science-fiction novel.

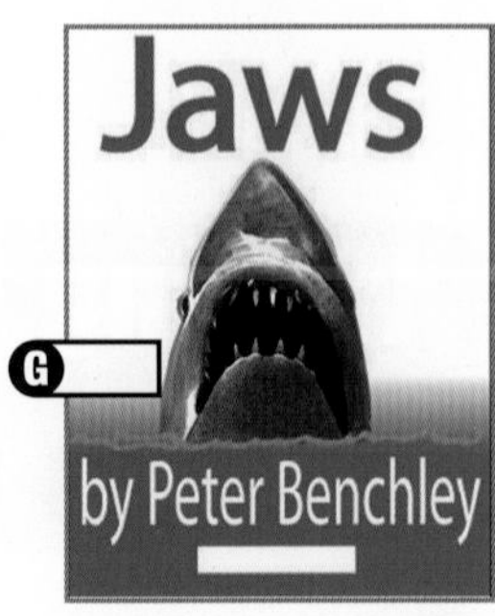

Reading and listening

Listen to Mark talking about his favourite Spielberg film and number the sentences in the correct order.

1 ☐ A man turns off the electricity.
2 ☐ The visitors escape on a helicopter.
3 ☐ A man builds a dinosaur park.
4 ☐ The children hide from two velociraptors.
5 ☐ Some visitors go to the island.
6 ☐ The dinosaurs escape and kill someone.

14 **3** **Listen to the story of Jurassic Park again and number the pictures in the correct order.**

Writing for your Portfolio

4 **Read the review of Jurassic Park. Did the writer like the film?**

I've just seen Jurassic Park. What a great film. I think it's the best film Spielberg has ever made. The story is really exciting. It's about some archaeologists who find some dinosaur blood in a mosquito. A businessman pays some scientists to use it and bring the animals back to life. They are successful and the businessman opens a theme park full of real dinosaurs. But before he can open the park to the public, some things start to go horribly wrong.

5 **Write a short review of a film that you have seen recently.**

Writing tip: reviews

- Start your review with your opinion of the film. Did you like it?
- Add a fact or two. Who directed it? Who are the actors?
- Tell the story. Only give a general idea of what happens. Don't give too many details and don't say what happens in the end!
- When we tell the story of films, books etc., we usually use the present simple tense.

....

....

....

....

Check your progress Units 1 and 2

1 Complete the names of the objects.

1 palm _ _ _
2 head _ _ _ _ _ _
3 MP3 p _ _ _ _ _
4 sun- _ _ _ _ _ _
5 digital c _ _ _ _ _
6 mobile p_ _ _ _

6

2 Complete the titles of the films.

1 w _ _ _ _ _ _
2 s _ _ _ _ _ _ f _ _ _ _ _ _
3 a _ _ _ _ _ _ _ _
4 w _ _
5 e _ _ _
6 c _ _ _ _ _ _

6

3 Complete the dialogues.

A [1]............. you ever .... (be) to Scotland?
B No, I [2] ....

A How long [3].......... he.......... (live) in England?
B He [4]............ ....(live) in England [5] .... four years.

A Have they [6]........ (see) their new house yet?
B Yes, they [7]....... already ....(move). I [8].......... (go) to see them yesterday!

8

4 Complete the sentences with the correct form of the Present perfect.

1 He ....(not / eat) anything yet.
2 We .... (know) him for years.
3 She .... (buy) a lot of things.
4 It .... (take) a lot of time.
5 I .... (not find) anything.

10

5 Write the questions.

1 ....
I think adventure films are exciting.
2 ....
Good idea! I'll take a picture and give it to my friend.
3 ....
I've always wanted to be a singer.
4 ....
Yes, he read the new Harry Potter book last week.
5 ....
No, I haven't done my English homework yet.

10

6 Complete the text with the correct form of the verb.

I [1].............. never .... (do) anything wrong but last year, I [2]................ (go) on holiday with some friends. We [3].............. (stay) in a resort with a lot of shops. One day, we [4].........(decide) to buy some souvenirs. I [5]..................... (not/have) any money so when no one was looking I [6] .... (take) a small souvenir. I [7].............. never .... (take) anything without paying before. I [8]............... (feel) terrible so I [9]............ (decide) to take it back. The next day I did and things were OK again. [10]............ you ever .... (think) of doing something wrong?

10

TOTAL 50

My progress so far is ...

brilliant! ☐ quite good. ☐ not great. ☐

Learn MORE about Culture

The European Union

1 How much do you know about the EU? Do our quick quiz and find out.

1 Which of these countries is not in the EU?
a) Portugal b) Sweden c) Switzerland

2 Which is the European Union flag?

3 Which of these member countries is the only one that uses the official currency, the Euro?
a) Denmark
b) Ireland
c) The UK

4 Where are the head offices of the EU?
a) Rome
b) Paris
c) Brussels

5 What is the population of the EU?
a) 200 million
b) 500 million
c) 900 million

Do YOU know?

The idea for the EEC (economic cooperation between European countries) came from a French Foreign Minister, Robert Shuman, in a speech on 9th May 1950. In 1992, after the signing of the Treaty of Maastricht, the EEC became the EU. This agreement started cooperation between European countries on defence and justice as well as on economics.

15 **2 Listen and decide if the sentences about EU regulations are true or false.**

1 There is a special European police force with members from all the countries in the European Union. T / F
2 The European Union wants labels on cosmetics and toiletries to be international so they may write the names of the ingredients in Latin. T / F
3 There are no TV advertisements for sweets and toys for children under twelve years old. T / F
4 It is illegal to sell peaches less than 56mm in diameter. T / F

MORE! And now you can watch *The School Magazine*! DVD

Casino Royale

What's the buzz?

Casino Royale, the new Bond film.

Who's in it?

Daniel Craig is Bond, James Bond. Eva Green is Bond girl Vesper Lynd and Dame Judi Dench is spymaster M.

What's it about?

Daniel Craig is the new James Bond. And the film makers have decided to make Bond more serious. This time we go back and look at Bond's early days as a super spy. This time Bond is up against super villain Le Chiffre. First he must play him in a game of poker and it's not just about money.

What's the best bit?

The chase scene in Madagascar is fantastic. This time Bond gets out of his car to run over walls, up and down cranes. It's completely different to anything you've seen in a Bond film before.

So is Daniel Craig any good?

Yes, he is. Daniel shows us just how good he's going to be. For the first time you can believe that Bond is a real person – not just some impossible superhero. He's so cool and he's great in the fight scenes.

What's the worst thing about it?

It's not as fun as other Bond films and that's because this Bond is more serious. There weren't a lot of laughs.

Hit or Miss?

Hit definitely. *Casino Royale* will keep old Bond fans happy but also attract new fans to the series. Daniel Craig has a bright future playing Britain's favourite spy.

But don't just take our word for it.

AMAZING! The best one yet! The Aston Martin DBS was such a cool car!
Sophie, 12, Reading

Easily the best Bond since Connery. Daniel Craig is a smashing new Bond with better cars and more evil villains. Definitely my favourite Bond.
Alex, 13, Stourbridge

Wow! Just got back from seeing it and it was great. I can't wait for the DVD.
Jack, 12, Liverpool

I think it was fantastic! I can't believe all the stunts they have in the film. I think he is a great new Bond!
Rosie, 12, Romford

I think the film is great. James' car is great!
Peter, 13, Rutherglen

I think that they could've done better with the car. But overall the film was good.
Sundeep, 12, Wolverhampton

For MORE! Go to www.cambridge.org/elt/more and do a quiz on this text.

UNIT 3 We're going to use it today

In this unit

You learn

- *will*
- *going to*
- reflexive pronouns
- words for geographical features

and then you can

- say what you are going to do
- talk about preferences
- talk about plans/offers

16 **1 Read and listen to the dialogue.**

Claire Hi, Rick. What's that?

Rick My new GPS unit. You know, Global Positioning System, like the one Dad's got in his car. We're going to use it today. Oliver and I are going to do some geocaching.

Claire Rick! Listen to yourself! Can you talk to me in English?

Rick Okay, I'll explain it. GPS is a system that tells you the way, it gives you directions.

Claire Yes, I know.

Rick Geocaching is a treasure hunt – you need a GPS unit, and the coordinates of the place where the treasure is. Then you go hunting – and that's what Oliver and I are going to do. We're really going to enjoy ourselves.

Claire And what's the treasure?

Rick Usually it's some small things in a box – a cache. If you find it, you can take something out but you must put something back in.

Claire So, you need to take some things with you. What are you going to take?

Rick I was thinking of your earrings!

Claire Very funny! So, where's Oliver?

Rick I don't know. I think I'll phone him.

Claire Maybe he's lost. Why don't you look for him with your GPS unit?

Rick Ha, ha. I won't even answer that!

2 **Match the sentence halves.**

1 Rick's dad has got GPS
2 Oliver and Rick are going to
3 Geocaching
4 For everything you take
5 Rick is thinking of
6 Oliver

a is a kind of treasure hunt.
b hasn't arrived yet.
c in his car.
d putting Claire's earrings into the box.
e use the GPS system to find a cache.
f out, you have to put something in.

Get talking Saying what you are going to do

17 **3** **Listen and repeat.**

A What are you going to do this afternoon?
B I'm not sure. I think I'll watch a film.

A Are you going to watch the match tonight?
B No, I can't. I'm going to study for tomorrow's biology test.

4 **Work with a partner. Ask and answer. Use the phrases and ideas below.**

Language Focus

Vocabulary Geographical features

18 **1 Listen. Then write the correct number next to the words on the left.**

- ☐ hill
- ☐ stars
- ☐ valley
- ☐ sea
- ☐ motorway
- ☐ town
- ☐ forest
- ☐ sun
- ☐ fields
- ☐ mountain
- ☐ road
- ☐ village
- ☐ lake
- ☐ river
- ☐ moon
- ☐ beach

Get talking Talking about preferences

19 **2 Complete the dialogues with the words on the left. Listen and check.**

road
cache
coordinates
forest
lake
hill

Mark So, where should we go now? Into the [1]............................ ?
Jill No, I'd rather go up the hill. I think the cache is up there.
Mark Are you sure? Read your [2]............................ again.
Jill Yes, I'm pretty sure. I don't want to go into the forest. I'd prefer to walk up the [3].....................

Helen Let's take the [4]............................ down the valley.
Archie I'd rather walk through the field. Then we can go down to the [5]............................
Helen No, not the field! I'd prefer to walk on a real road.
Archie But a [6]............................ is never so close to the road!

3 Work with a partner. Ask and answer. Change roles.

A Would you like to go to the sea?

B I'd prefer / I'd rather go to …

Leisure time

go to the cinema – go to a club
play football – play tennis
watch TV – go for a walk

Holiday

the sea – the mountains
England – Spain
the beach – the lake

Grammar

will

1 **I'll** explain it. 2 **I'll** help you. 3 I think **I'll** phone him

1 **Match the examples with the rules.**

We use *will* to:

a) make offers - ....

b) make decisions (usually at the same time as speaking) - ....

2 **Complete the sentences. Use *will* and the verb in brackets.**

1 'This work's very hard!' 'Don't worry – I'll help... you.' (help)
2 'Where's Sheila?' 'I don't know. .... her.' (phone)
3 'It's hot in here!' 'OK. .... the window if you like.' (open)
4 'I'm thirsty.' 'OK. .... some orange juice.' (make)
5 'I haven't got enough money for an ice cream.' 'That's OK. .... one for you.' (buy)
6 'I don't understand this!' 'It's OK – .... it to you.' (explain)

going to

3 **Put the words in the correct order then check in the dialogue on page 24.**

Rick: and / I / geocaching / to / going / are / do / Oliver / some
Claire: are / What / you / going / with / to / you? / take.

We use *be going to* to talk and ask about intentions and things we have already decided to do.

4 **Write sentences using the correct form of *be going to* and a verb from the right.**

~~buy~~
give
see
be

1 My parents' car is very old, so they're going to buy a new one.
2 When my brother leaves school, he .... a doctor.
3 It's my sister's birthday next week, and I .... her a really nice present.
4 Next Monday is a holiday and we .... our grandparents.

5 **Circle the correct answer.**

1 **A** Sorry – we haven't got orange juice.
B (decides now) OK. (I'll) / *I'm going to* have milk.
2 **A** Is that DVD good?
B (decided before) No. *I'll / I'm going to* watch a different one.
3 **A** Do you want to go out?
B (decided before) No, *I'll / I'm going to* finish my homework.
4 **A** I need to surf the internet.
B (decides now) OK. *I'll / I'm going to* switch the computer on.

Sounds right *going to*

6 **When we say *going to*, it often sounds like *gonna*. Listen and repeat.**

I'm going to write a letter.
I'm going to put it in the post.
And the letter's going to tell you
That I miss you the most.

Reflexive pronouns

7 **Look at the dialogue on page 24 and complete the examples.**

Rick! Listen to ....
We're really going to enjoy ....

When the subject and the object of a verb are the same, we use 'reflexive pronouns' as the object, for example: Stop talking to yourself!

We can also use reflexive pronouns if we want to emphasise something about the subject, for example: She doesn't want any help – **she** wants to do it (**herself**).

8 **Complete with the correct reflexive pronoun.**

Subject pronouns	Reflexive pronouns
I	myself
you	1 ....
he	himself
she	2 ....
it	itself
we	3 ....
you	yourselves
they	themselves

9 **Complete with the correct reflexive pronoun.**

1 We're going to decorate our room *ourselves.*
2 Be careful, Mike! You're going to hurt .... !
3 She enjoyed .... at the party.
4 My parents are going to buy .... some new clothes.
5 He's a strange person – he always talks to ....
6 I'm going to cook dinner .... tonight.
7 My cat washes .... all the time.
8 Bye, Alan! Bye, Susan! I hope you enjoy .... tonight!

Get talking Talking about plans/offers

21 **10** **Complete the dialogue with the correct phrases. Then listen and check.**

you're going to start
I'm going to hide some things
What are you going to hide there

Marina 1 .... in our cache near the lake.
Chris Can I come along?
Marina Sure. Does that mean 2 .... geocaching, too?
Chris I don't think so. 3 ....anyway?
Marina Oh, a couple of books and a video of our last geocaching hunt.
Chris Are people interested in things like that?
Marina I hope so!

Reading

Read the story.

TREASURE HUNT

When Dad said that Gillie and I could go to an adventure holiday camp, I wasn't too excited. I didn't want to go away with my twelve-year-old sister! But I was wrong – Gillie was OK.

The best thing were the surprise activities: wild-water canoeing, rock climbing, and a visit to the waterfall. And our guides were fantastic. Especially Ron. He was really cool.

One Friday, Gillie was very excited: "Chris, come quickly, there's a geocaching treasure hunt with Ron tomorrow. But only 20 kids can go!"

"Geocaching???" I thought. I had no idea what it was, but I didn't want to ask her. I'm fourteen, and she's twelve, you know.

I asked Ron about geocaching. It sounded great, so Gillie and I signed up.

Geocaching treasure hunt!
When: Wednesday 1pm
Bring: good shoes, a snack and a bottle of water.
Don't forget: one or two small things for the cache!
Write your name on the list – only 20 kids can go!
See you! Ron

The next day we started our geocaching hunt. For three hours we looked everywhere; behind every tree, under every stone, in every hole in the ground. Nothing! Then suddenly Gillie shouted: "Here it is!" She had her hand in a hole in the ground, but when she took it out, I knew that it wasn't the "cache" box with a small surprise present in it. My twelve-year-old sister had a handful of old coins!

We showed the coins to Ron and he laughed. "Old coins? Very funny! They're not old. But give them to me." Ron was very nice. He gave me a *Scissor Sisters* CD and my sister a bar of chocolate for the coins. Later in the evening, Gillie showed me a coin. "I didn't give him this one," she said. "I wanted to keep it." Two days later we went on a trip to a museum near our camp with Ron. We saw lots of interesting things. Suddenly Gillie shouted, "Look at those coins! They look like my coin!" She had the coin in her hand and it looked exactly like the old Roman coins behind the glass window. One of the men in uniform heard Gillie. He walked towards us. When Ron saw him, he got very nervous. "Where did you find this coin?", the man asked. "In the forest," Gillie replied. "We found lots of them. But we gave them to him!"

Gillie pointed at Ron. Suddenly Ron turned and ran away! The man in uniform phoned the police. Two policemen came and took us to the police station. "These coins are Roman," one of them said, "When you find old coins, you have to give them to the museum. We're going to find this Ron. He can't keep the coins!"

Two days later the police found Ron. They took the coins away from him. Now they're behind glass in the museum. And next to them there's a little sign:

ROMAN COINS (AD 42)
FOUND BY
GILLIE WOODHOUSE

Gillie's very proud of this. Well, after all, she's only twelve.

2 **Match the sentence halves.**

1 Gillie and her brother Chris
2 They really liked the
3 One day they took part in a
4 Chris and his sister didn't find the cache,
5 Ron laughed when the children showed
6 Two days later the children went
7 They found out that their coins were
8 The police caught Ron and

a surprise activities.
b but they found some coins.
c him the coins.
d went to an adventure holiday camp.
e very old.
f geocaching hunt with a guide called Ron.
g took the coins away from him.
h to a museum.

Listening

22 **3** **Listen to Sarah talking about the adventure camp she went to. Circle T (true) or F (false) for the sentences below.**

1 Sarah went rock climbing and canoeing. T / F
2 It was her first time in a canoe. T / F
3 Her canoe was for one person. T / F
4 Sarah couldn't get out of the water herself. T / F
5 She hurt herself. T / F
6 She didn't go canoeing again. T / F

Sounds right Stress in compound nouns

23 **4** **When a word is made up of two nouns, we usually stress the first noun more. Listen and repeat. Match the words to make compound nouns.**

rock climbing

rock	riding
class	fall
adventure	work
home	climbing
water	camp
motor	room
horse	way
treasure	hunt

5 **Work with a partner. Make dialogues.**

A What are you going to do at the weekend?

B I'm going to go rock climbing.

Speaking

6 **Here are six activities you can do at an adventure camp. Number them 1- 6: 1 = the activity you think is best, 6 = the activity you think is worst.**

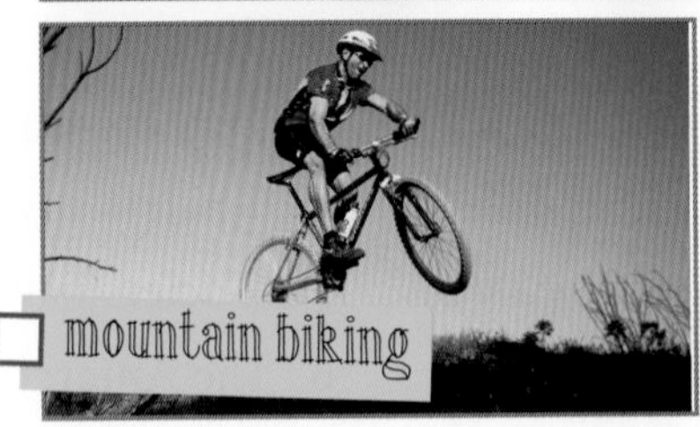

7 **Work in groups of three. Discuss three activities for the group to do.**

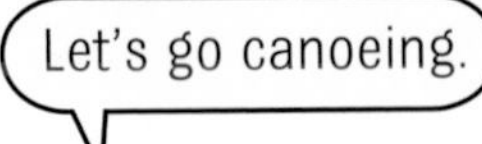

No, that's boring / too difficult!

I'd prefer to ...

Writing for your Portfolio

8 **Imagine you are at an adventure camp. Choose some of the activities from exercise 6 and write a postcard to a friend. Tell him / her:**

- if you are enjoying yourself
- what you did yesterday
- what you are going to do for the rest of your holiday

Glaciers

Key words

melts	shrinking	sensation	compressed	a large mass of ice
flow	mummy	resources	masses of snow	carved out valleys

24 **1** **Do the quiz about glaciers. Underline the correct solution. Then listen and check.**

1 Glaciers today are getting *smaller/bigger*.
2 We can call glaciers *lakes/rivers* of ice.
3 Very big glaciers can be *40/80* km long.
4 Glaciers cover about *2%/10%* of the Earth's land area.
5 Glaciers have *75%/25%* of the Earth's fresh water.
6 The Antarctic ice is about *4000/400* metres thick in some places.
7 Most of the glaciers in the USA are in *California/Alaska*.
8 Are there glaciers in every continent? *Yes/No*.

2 **Read the text about glaciers.**

What are glaciers? Glaciers are masses of snow that have become ice. Sometimes, when snow falls and stays on the ground long enough, it is compressed over many years into a large mass of ice, and that is a glacier.
Glaciers are great rivers of ice. Their own weight makes glaciers flow like very slow rivers. For millions of years, moving glaciers have formed mountains and carved out valleys. They continue to flow and form the landscape in many places.
But today there is a big problem. Glaciers are shrinking fast because the world is getting warmer. This is true in almost every region of the world. An American professor found some plants near a glacier in Peru. Scientists found that the plants were about 5000 years old. The ice of the glacier covered them for all that time, but when the glacier got smaller, the plants appeared again.

In 1991 hikers found a mummy in the Alps at a height of 3210 metres. It was a sensation. Scientists discovered that the man crossed the glacier about 5300 years ago, then snow and ice covered him for thousands of years. But as the weather got warmer and the ice melted, the famous Iceman appeared.

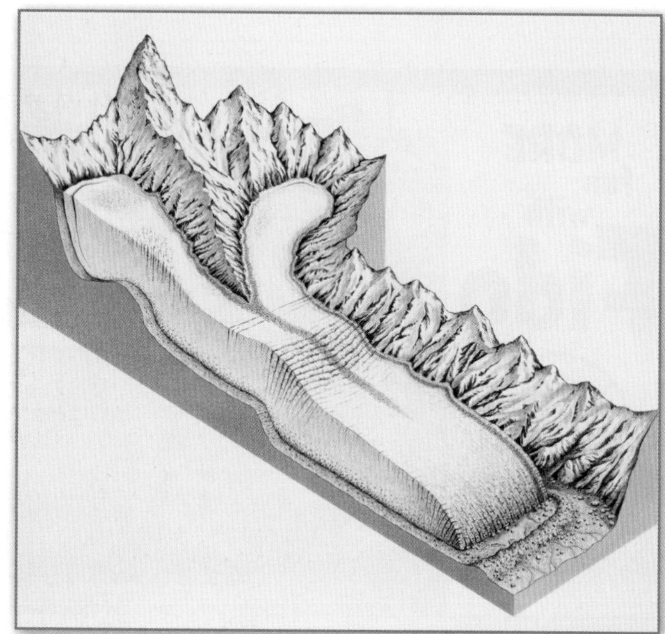

3 **Compare the photos below.**

1875

Today

In many countries, glaciers are major resources for hydroelectric power production. They are also very important for watering the fields and for providing drinking water for cities. But now, as the ice melts, glaciers all over the world will move up the mountains and get smaller.
Perhaps the biggest problem is this: what is going to happen to all the ice in Greenland and the Antarctic? If the huge masses of ice melt and flow into the ocean, then the level of the water of the ocean will go up. Nobody knows how far. But you can imagine that people living on islands, only one or two metres above sea level, are very worried.
Australian scientists found that the sea level rose about 20 cm between 1807 and 2004. Other scientists say that sea levels could rise between 10cm and 1 metre by the year 2100.

The leaders of Tuvalu – a tiny island country in between Hawaii and Australia – want to leave their islands in the future. During the twentieth century, the sea level rose by 20-30 centimetres. Scientists say that a rise of up to 1 metre during this century is possible. As the sea level has risen, the fields on Tuvalu have been flooded by salt water. This means that people do not have fresh water to drink any more, and that they cannot water their vegetables in the fields.

Mini-project Rising sea levels

4 **Check the internet or in the library for facts and idea about rising sea levels.**

UNIT 4 Superstitions!

1 **Are you superstitious? Read about amazing superstitions from all over the world.**

There are many weird and wonderful **SUPERSTITIONS** all over the world. Look at these, for example:

CHINA

On New Year's Day, dirt should not be swept out of the house because this will sweep out good luck too. After the first of January dirt should only be swept out of the back of the house.

THAILAND

Do not tell other people about your bad dream when you are eating. If you do, your dream will come true.

BRAZIL

Many Brazilians believe that you will have money all year if you eat lentils on the first of January. So don't forget to eat lots of lentils at the beginning of the new year.

KOREA

Some Koreans believe if you see a magpie in the morning, you'll get good news.

ARGENTINA

If you come across some money on the pavement, pick it up because you'll get more money. When you're walking along the street in Argentina you should be extra careful. There might be people looking at the ground and not at the traffic. Try not to walk into them.

And what **SUPERSTITIONS** do you believe in?

In this unit

You learn

- prepositions
- common verbs plus prepositions
- phrasal verbs
- words for star signs

and then you can

- talk about superstitions
- talk about star signs
- find out about people

2 **Complete the statements about superstitions with the correct information from the text.**

1 In China, if you sweep dirt out of the house on New Year's Day ...
2 Some people in Argentina believe they will get rich if ...
3 Some Brazilians believe that if you eat lentils on ...
5 If you want good news in Korea, you must see ...
6 In Thailand, if you tell people about your bad dream while eating, ...

Get talking Talking about superstitions

25 **3** **Listen and repeat.**

A What will happen if I look at the moon at midnight?
B You will meet someone special.

A What will happen if I dream of flying?
B You will go abroad very soon.

4 **Work in pairs. Invent different superstitions. Use the pictures below. A chooses three pictures and B chooses three sentences. Change over.**

A What will happen if you look at the moon?
B You will find some money.

look at the moon

break a mirror

see two black cats

dream about the sea

find a button

think about the Queen

You will make a new friend.
You will have a bad day.
You will go on a long journey.
You will visit London very soon.
You will get a wonderful present.
You will win a lot of money.

Language Focus

Vocabulary Star signs

ARIES
March 21 – April 19

LEO
July 21 – August 22

SAGITTARIUS
November 22 – December 21

TAURUS
April 20 – May 20

VIRGO
August 23 – September 22

CAPRICORN
December 22 – January 19

GEMINI
May 21 – June 20

LIBRA
September 23 – October 22

AQUARIUS
January 20 – February 18

CANCER
June 21 – July 20

SCORPIO
October 23 – November 21

PISCES
February 19 – March 20

26 **1 Listen and write the names of the star signs.**

1 A .... is very friendly and gets on very well with other people.
2 .... are happy people. They always smile and laugh a lot.
3 A .... is very determined and always gets what they want.
4 A .... is very energetic, works hard and is busy all the time.
5 .... are very helpful. They have lots of friends.
6 .... are very intelligent. They love solving all kinds of problems.
7 .... are very romantic. They like love stories.
8 .... are very dynamic. They love to keep fit and do all kinds of sports.
9 .... are very passionate. They feel very positive about what they do.
10 A .... is very flexible and can do more than one thing at the same time.
11 An .... is very positive and always sees the good side of life.
12 A .... is a very generous person and likes giving presents.

Get talking Talking about star signs

27 **2 Listen and repeat.**

A What star sign are you?
B I'm Leo.
A Are you a typical Leo?
B Yes, I am. I have lots of friends. / No, I'm not. I'm …

3 Work in pairs. Make similar dialogues to Exercise 2.

Grammar

Prepositions

1 **Complete the examples with prepositions then check in the text on page 34.**

... eat lentils [1]............................. the first of January.
... see a magpie [2]............................. the morning.
... some money [3]............................. the pavement.
... dirt should not be swept [4]............................. of the house.
... lots of lentils [5]............................. the beginning of the new year.
... walking [6]............................. the street.

2 **Look back at the prepositions in the examples. Which refer to:**

a) time? b) place? c) movement?

3 **Complete the sentences with the correct preposition.**

1 There's a clock .... the wall behind you.
2 Let's meet .... three o'clock .... Thursday.
3 I saw him run .... the road and .... the bridge.
4 I'm not walking .... that mountain! It's too high.
5 The bank is .... to the cinema, opposite the supermarket.
6 I was born .... the spring – .... March 22nd.
7 He rode his bike .... a wall and fell off.
8 The cat's under the table .... the dining room.

Common verbs + prepositions

Some verbs are followed by certain prepositions.

tell someone **about** something
look **at** the ground
What superstitions do you believe **in**?

4 **Choose the correct preposition to complete the sentences.**

1 Tony! I was just thinking *for/about/in* you.
2 What time do you wake *up/out/into* in the morning?
3 Turn *up/through/down* the TV. It's too loud.
4 Come in and sit *down/up/into*.
5 Let me pay *over/in/for* this meal.
6 I'm excited *for/about/in* going on holiday!
7 Do you usually tell him *for/about/on* things?
8 Did you read *for/about/in* the new film?

5 **Complete the sentences with the correct preposition.**

at (x3) with (x3) for on ~~up~~

1 I want you to tidy ...up..... your bedroom, now!
2 What do you see when you look .... the sky?
3 Turn .... the TV. There's a good film starting.
4 Why are you laughing .... me? What did I do?
5 She lives .... dad and I live .... mum.
6 I'm sorry but I don't agree .... you.
7 I want to apologise .... being rude. I'm sorry.
8 He's good .... everything!

Phrasal verbs

6 **Look at the example and answer the question.**

If you *come across* some money on the pavement, pick it up
What does *come across* mean?

a) walk on b) drop c) find

Sometimes the meaning of a verb changes completely because of the preposition which follows it. These are known as phrasal verbs.

7 **Circle the phrasal verbs and match them to the correct meaning.**

1 No thanks, I've given up eating chocolate. - e
2 The police are looking into the robbery.
3 They've put off their wedding until May.
4 He takes after his father. He really likes sport too.
5 I bumped into Jim. I haven't seen him for weeks.
6 We made up the exercise.

a postpone to a later date
b behaves the same as
c meet by chance (not planned)
d invent
e stop
f investigate

Get talking Finding out about people

28 **8** **Complete the dialogues with the correct phrasal verbs. Then listen and check.**

A I saw Mark yesterday.
B Oh, how is he?
A Fantastic! He [1]..................... smoking.
He looks very fit and healthy!
B Good for him!

A Guess what happened to me this morning?
B You won the lottery.
A No! I [2]..................... Sally outside the bank.
B Sally! I haven't seen her for ages.

9 **Work in pairs. How well do you know your partner? Complete the sentences.**

1 He/she is interested in ...
2 He/she likes listening to ...
3 He/she is thinking about ...
4 On Sundays he/she gets up at ...
5 He/she enjoys reading about ...
6 He/she likes talking to ...
7 He/she's very good at ...
8 He/she spends a lot of money on ...

10 **Now check with your partner.**

A Are you interested in animals?
B Yes, I am. / No, I'm not.

B Do you like listening to rap music?
A Yes, I do. / No, I don't.

Skills

Listening and reading

1 Read and listen to scenes 1, 2 and 3 of the play.

The Ancient Coin

Mr Morris

Scene 1

Neil How long was John in India?

Mrs Morris About five years. And do you know what? He brought back an ancient coin.

Neil A coin? An ancient coin? What for?

Mr Morris You can ask him. [*The doorbell rings*] Here he is!

Mrs Morris

Scene 2

Neil Why did you bring an ancient coin from India?

John Well, if you make a wish and hold the ancient coin in your hand, your wish will come true.

Neil Wow! How many wishes can you make with it?

John Three. Here it is. Look at it. You can have the coin. I don't want it any more.

Mrs Morris Why not?

John I'm scared of it. I'm afraid that it will bring bad luck. Keep the coin Neil – but don't make a wish. I think it might be dangerous.

Neil OK, don't worry.

Neil

Scene 3

Neil Wow. I've got the ancient coin. Now I can make a wish!

Mrs Morris No, Neil! Don't!

Neil Come on, Mum! We've got three wishes. If the first wish brings us bad luck, we'll have two more wishes for good luck.

Mrs Morris Neil, I don't think you should do this.

Neil Oh, come on, Mum!

Mr Morris Give me the coin. I'll make the wish. Here we go. I wish for £50,000.

John

2 Complete the sentences.

1 John was in India for .... years.
2 He brought a .... from India.
3 If you hold the coin when you make a wish, your wish ....
4 John is scared the coin will bring ....
5 He gives it to ....
6 Neil's father wishes for ....

30 **3** **Listen to scenes 4 and 5. Match the sentence halves.**

1 Neil phones his dad and
2 He has won £50,000
3 Neil says that he
4 When the doorbell rings, Neil's parents think that
5 But it isn't their son,
6 He tells Mr and Mrs Morris that

a it's a policeman.
b it's their son.
c their son had an accident.
d will be home in half an hour.
e in the lottery.
f tells him some great news.

31 **4** **Listen to scene 6. Put the lines into the correct order to write a summary on a piece of paper.**

Then Mr. Morris wishes for £50,000.
3 John gives the ancient coin to Neil.
1 Mr. Morris tells his family about an ancient coin. Then John Williams arrives.
Mr Morris throws the coin into the fire. A doctor phones and tells them that Neil is fine.
Three days later, Neil phones and says that he has won the lottery.
2 He shows them the coin and says, "If you make a wish, the wish will come true".
Neil wants to make a wish, but his Mum stops him.
A policeman arrives and says that Neil had an accident.

Writing for your Portfolio

5 **Read the text about the Ancient Coin. Which parts do you agree/disagree with?**

The Ancient Coin is a mystery story. I love mystery stories so I really wanted to read it. Luckily I wasn't disappointed. I thought it was very good. The beginning was great. The idea of a coin that makes wishes come true is very interesting. I would love one! I wasn't surprised that Mr Morris wished for money. A lot of people would make the same wish, I'm sure. The best bit was when the policemen tells them about Neil's accident. I was sure he was dead. The only bit I didn't like was the end. I wanted the family to make another wish.

6 **Think of a story you have read or heard recently. Write a short text saying what you thought about it.**

Writing tips Giving opinions and justifying them

Before you write, think about the following things:

- Were you interested by the story before you started reading it? Did it disappoint you?
- Which were the best bits? Why did you like them?
- Which bits (if any) weren't so good? What was wrong with them?

Remember – every time you give an opinion, write another sentence to explain your opinion.

Check your progress Units 3 and 4

1 Complete the sentences.

1 I climbed to the top of the h _ _ _ .
2 There are bright s _ _ _ _ in the sky.
3 The M40 is a m _ _ _ _ _ _ _ near London.
4 The m _ _ _ was shining last night.
5 The f _ _ _ _ was full of flowers.
6 There was a l _ _ _ with lots of fish. ☐ 6

2 Read the descriptions and complete the sentences.

1 He gets on well with other people. He's f _ _ _ _ _ _ _ .
2 She likes watching love stories. She's r _ _ _ _ _ _ _ .
3 He likes giving presents. He's g _ _ _ _ _ _ _ .
4 She does a lot and is busy all the time. She's e _ _ _ _ _ _ _ _ .
5 He always gets what he wants. He's very d _ _ _ _ _ _ _ _ .
6 She always passes her exams. She's very i _ _ _ _ _ _ _ _ _ _ . ☐ 6

3 Complete the dialogues. Use *be going to* or *will*.

A What [1]............... he .... (do) tomorrow?
B He's [2]............. (see) some friends .
A [3]............ you .... (visit) them too?
B I'm not sure. I think I [4]............... (decide) tomorrow.

A Which pen would you like?
B I [5]............ (take) that one, please!

A Amanda and I [6]................ (have a party) on Saturday.
B [7]............ Mike .... (come)?
A I don't know. I [8]......... (call) him tomorrow.

☐ 8

4 Complete the sentences with a reflexive pronoun.

1 They enjoyed .... at the festival.
2 We're going to cook dinner ....
3 Don't hurt .... ! Be careful!
4 She decorated the living room ....

☐ 4

5 Complete the sentences with a preposition.

1 He always arrives .... night.
2 They ran .... the road in front of a car.
3 She works .... the morning.
4 We are walking .... the mountain to the top.
5 She takes .... her father. They are very similar.
6 My desk is in front of Sarah's desk. She sits .... me.
7 We're going to leave .... Monday.
8 He wasn't looking and walked .... a policeman.
9 She made .... that story. It wasn't true!
10 I'll see him .... dinner. ☐ 10

6 Write the questions.

1 ....
I'd prefer to go to the sea not the mountains.
2 ....
On Saturday, I'm going to visit my aunt.
3 ....
I'm a Leo.
4 ....
No, I'm not going to see Mark tomorrow.
5 ....
Yes, I am interested in science. ☐ 10

7 Complete the text with a preposition.

Mark was thinking [1]................ his friend Sarah yesterday. He wanted to apologise [2]............ being rude. When he saw her last week, she was excited [3]............ going on holiday. He laughed [4]......... Sarah and turned [5]........... the TV so he didn't have to talk to her. This time he is going to pay [6]................ a meal for both of them! ☐ 6

TOTAL ☐ 50

My progress so far is ...

brilliant! ☐ quite good. ☐ not great. ☐

Modern Books and writers

1 **Read the extracts from the books and answer the questions. Remember you don't need to understand all the words in the text.**

LEVEL 4 - Kid City

By Andreas Schlüter

Ben told her the rules of his computer game. "Don't you see," he went on. "In the computer game, everyone older than fifteen disappears. And that's exactly what's happened here in this city!"

"You mean your computer game has turned real?"

"It may sound crazy but yes, that's exactly what I mean."

(A) "You're round the twist!"

1 How do you think Jennifer and Ben feel?
2 Why do they feel like this?

The Blood Stone

By Jamila Gavin

"If this is the house of Geronimo Veroneo, I have a message for you, but let me in for I must speak with you in private. There is danger for all of us." The voice was foreign, (B) the words used a mixture of Italian and Venetian, so broken and guttural that they could only barely understand him. Carlo listened, (C) frozen by indecision. Then Teodora's (D) anguished whisper broke through their trance. "Let him in Carlo, let him in."

"No mother. It could be a trick. We need proof.

1 Do you think the man has come to help them or to hurt them?

2 **Read the extracts again and match the underlined sections with the words and phrases below.**

1 it was difficult to understand him because he spoke very badly ☐
2 not able to decide what to do ☐
3 frightened and worried ☐
4 You're mad. ☐

32 **3** **Listen to the interview with the Indian author of *The Blood Stone*, Jamila Gavin. Then answer the questions.**

1 When did she move to England?
2 Why didn't she like school?
3 Where did she work after she left the Guildhall School of Music?
4 Who did she write her books for?
5 What is the location of her new book?

4 **Over 2 U!** **Work with a partner and talk about your favourite book. Discuss the title, author, characters and storyline. Say why you like the book.**

One of the bestselling children's books in English of all time is a little book called *Charlotte's Web* about a small spider, a girl and a pig.

MORE! And now you can watch *The School Magazine!* DVD

Two wishes

It was the day before the most important exam of the year. Maths! I hate maths. I just don't understand it. Numbers don't make any sense. Give me words. I love words.

I was looking at my book on the desk and trying to revise. But I just didn't understand it. I kept thinking about my birthday on Friday. Fail my maths exam and goodbye party. I was depressed. My birthday! Then I remembered, don't you get one wish for every birthday? Could I make my wish now, three days early?

I looked at my book and I made a wish. I wished for the best birthday party ever and then I made a second wish. I wished that for once I could get the best mark in the class. Better than Kate Holmes, better than James Love, better than all those clever kids who always get the top marks.

Then I went to bed. I was tired from all the wishing.

The next day I woke up and went to school. I was nervous. It was exam day and I didn't know anything. I hoped my birthday wish would work. I took my picture of my dog with me and put it on the desk. It's my lucky charm and it always brings me good luck.

Miss Chappell, the maths teacher gave me my exam. I looked at it. Was this maths? It looked like Greek to me, all those symbols and strange letters. Luckily it was multiple choice. I put circles around the A, B and Cs and spent the rest of the exam thinking about my party.

The next day I got to school I was really nervous. Results. Was this the end of my party? We got to the classroom but Miss Chappell was not there. The headmaster arrived. Miss C was ill. The results would be on Monday. I was free!

The party was great. Everyone was there. Kate Holmes and James Love talked about the maths exam all night. I didn't care. I just danced.

So did the wish come true? I had the best party ever, that's true. Well remember that I said you get one wish every birthday. Well, I made two. And the second wish? Well on Monday morning Miss C was there. I got my results. 33.33% exactly. Bottom of the class. Yes, it was that bad!

Read the story again and put the following events in the correct order.

- ☐ She had a great time at the party.
- ☐ She did her exam.
- ☐ She failed the maths exam.
- ☐ She went to bed.
- ☐ She made a birthday wish.
- ☐ She got her results.
- 1 Jenny was trying to revise.
- ☐ Her teacher was ill.

For MORE! Go to www.cambridge.org/elt/more and do a quiz on this text.

UNIT 5 It's easy, isn't it?

In this unit

You learn
- relative pronouns *who/which/that*
- question tags
- words for places

and then you can
- ask for information at the cinema
- ask for more information

33 **1 Read and listen to the dialogue.**

Claire This London quiz isn't easy, is it? Question 8: 'What's the name of the tower that is 98 metres high?' The answer's Big Ben, isn't it?

Karen No, you're wrong. Big Ben isn't the tower, and it isn't the clock – it's the bell!

Claire How do you know that?

Karen I did a bit of Internet research before you came. I think the answer is the Telecom Tower. OK, next question. 'What's the name of the art gallery which is in an old factory building?' That's easy. It's the Tate Modern.

Claire The only question I can answer is the one about the man who built St. Paul's Cathedral! That's Christopher Wren.

Karen Thank goodness for the Internet!

Claire Mr Collins wants this tomorrow, doesn't he?

Karen Yeah. So come on, let's finish it. Rick'll be here any minute to pick us up.

(A few minutes later)

Rick Hi. Are you ready to go? Have you finished the assignment about London?

Claire Yes, we have. I bet you haven't finished it, have you?

Rick No, I didn't have time. Could you email me the answers?

Karen Only if you buy us an ice cream at the cinema!

2 **Circle T (True) or F (False) for the sentences below.**

1 Claire thinks the London quiz is difficult. T / F
2 The name of the clock in the tower is Big Ben. T / F
3 In London they turned an old factory into an art gallery. T / F
4 Their teacher wants the answers to the quiz the next day. T / F
5 Rick hasn't finished the assignment about London. T / F

Get talking Asking for information at the cinema

34 **3** **Listen and repeat.**

Girl Excuse me, what film is on Screen 10?
Assistant *Chocoholics*. Would you like a ticket?

Boy Excuse me, the main film hasn't started yet, has it?
Assistant No, they're still showing the trailers.

Girl You've still got tickets for the new Spielberg film, haven't you?
Assistant No, sorry! They sold out hours ago.

35 **4** **Match the questions and answers. Then listen and check.**

Questions
1 Have you still got tickets for the 9.00 show?
2 How much is a student ticket?
3 What kind of film is *Eternal Sunshine*?
4 Can I sit anywhere I like?
5 How long is the main film?

Answers
a It's a comedy, but some parts are sad too.
b Let me see – it's about 89 minutes.
c Yes, we've got lots.
d It's £4. But you need some identification.
e Of course you can.

5 **Work in pairs. Practise the dialogues from Exercise 4.**

Language Focus

Vocabulary Places

36 **1** **Listen and write the words under the pictures.**

theatre
castle
park
exhibition
museum
megastore
market
cinema
aquarium
concert

1 .... 2 .... 3 .... 4 .... 5 ....

6 .... 7 .... 8 .... 9 .... 10 ....

Get talking Asking for more information

37 **2** **Complete the dialogues with the sentences. Listen and check. Act them out.**

Yes, it is. I think it's open from 12-6.
I'm afraid we don't.
Yes, we have. How many do you want?
How much are they?
I'm pretty sure, but we can phone them.

At the theatre box office

Natasha Excuse me, have you got any tickets left for tonight's performance?
Assistant [1] ....
Natasha Two please.
Assistant OK – I've got two tickets in the 2nd row.
Natasha [2] ....
Assistant £10 each.
Natasha Do you do any reductions for students?
Assistant I'm sorry – [3] ....
Natasha Alright. I'll take them anyway.

Fred Is the record store open on Sundays?
Ken [4] ....
Fred Are you sure? I don't want to go there and find it's closed.
Ken [5] ....

3 **Work with a partner. Pick a place/an event from Exercise 1 and make up a dialogue. Ask about opening times, tickets, prices and reductions.**

Grammar

Relative pronouns *who / which / that*

1 **Complete the examples then check with the dialogue on page 44.**

What's the name of the tower [1] .... is 98 metres high?
What's the name of the art gallery [2] .... is in an old factory building?
Christopher Wren was the man [3] .... built St Paul's Cathedral.

We use the relative pronouns *who / that* to talk about people.
We use the relative pronouns *which / that* to talk about animals and things.

2 **Circle the correct word.**

1 I've got a friend *who / which* hates pizza!
2 That's the restaurant *who / which* has the best food in town!
3 An atlas is a book *who / which* gives you information about different countries.
4 I like people *who / which* give me presents.
5 Alison's the girl *which / that* always comes first in our class.
6 I never buy clothes *who / that* are very expensive.

3 **Complete the definitions.**

A
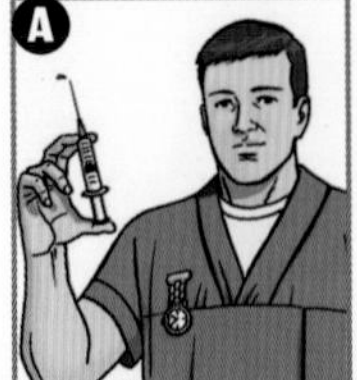
B
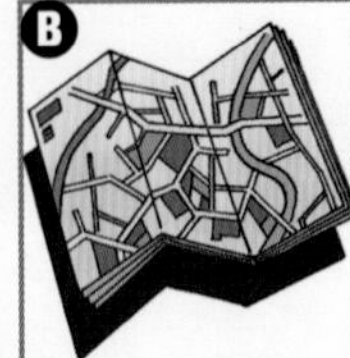
C

D

E

1 A nurse is a person *who helps sick people in hospital.*
2 A map is a thing ....
3 A magnifying glass is a thing ....
4 A sheepdog is an animal ....
5 A traffic warden is a person ....

4 **Make one sentence from two.**

1 A programmer is a person. He / She writes programs for computers.
A programmer is a person who / that writes programs for computers.
2 A dictionary is a book. It tells you the meanings of words.
....
....
3 A pilot is a person. He / She flies planes.
....
....
4 A megastore is a shop. It sells almost everything.
....
....
5 Ferraris are Italian cars. They are very expensive.
....
....

Question tags

5 **Look at the dialogue on page 44 and complete the examples.**

1 This London quiz isn't easy, ... ?
2 The answer's Big Ben, ... ?

With positive statements we usually use a negative question tag.
With negative statements, we usually use a positive question tag.
Question tags are commonly used to confirm information or to invite the listener to agree.

6 **Complete the sentences with the question tags below.**

aren't you | does she | wasn't it | didn't we | won't you | doesn't she

1 You aren't English, *are you*.. ?
2 It was cold there, ... ?
3 You'll help me, ... ?
4 She speaks English, ... ?
5 You're going to be at the party, ... ?
6 We enjoyed ourselves, ... ?
7 Your sister doesn't like me, ... ?

7 **Complete the sentences with the question tags below.**

does she | didn't you | has he | aren't they | will it

1 He hasn't gone, ... ?
2 She doesn't live in Rome, ... ?
3 They are Italian, ... ?
4 You went to London last year, ... ?
5 It won't happen, ... ?

Sounds right Intonation in question tags

38 **8** **When we are sure about something, our intonation goes down at the end. When we are unsure, our intonation goes up at the end. Listen and repeat the sentences then circle (U) for unsure and (S) for sure.**

1 It's cold today, isn't it? U / S
2 You don't like me, do you? U / S
3 They're nice people, aren't they? U / S
4 I'm not late, am I? U / S
5 You didn't forget, did you? U / S
6 It isn't wrong, is it? U / S

Skills

Reading

1 Read the text

The Great Fire of London

In the 17th century, London was a city of narrow streets and wooden houses. On the evening of Sunday, September 2, 1666, a fire began in a house near London Bridge. The wind was strong, and the fire grew and grew. It went on during Monday and Tuesday.

A famous writer called Samuel Pepys was living in London at that time. He wrote this in his diary:

> 'I went out, and walked to the Tower. There I saw all the houses at the end of the bridge on fire. The people of the Tower told me that the fire started in the King's baker's house in Pudding Lane. It has already burned down a church and most of Fish Street. Everybody is trying to move their things, or throwing them into the river or taking them to boats.'

On Wednesday, the fire got weaker, and on Thursday 6 September, it stopped completely. In those four days, the fire destroyed old St Paul's Cathedral, 87 other churches and about 13,000 houses – about 80% of the city at that time. But amazingly, only about 15 people died.

King Charles II decided to build London again, with wider streets and houses built of brick, not wood. One of the men who rebuilt the city was Christopher Wren, a great architect. His most famous building was the new St Paul's Cathedral, which is still there now.

Near St Paul's, you can also see 'The Monument', a column built in the 1670s to remember the Great Fire. It is very close to the place where the fire began.

2 Circle T (True) or F (False) for the sentences below.

1 In 1666, streets in London were not wide. T / F
2 The fire began in a church. T / F
3 Samuel Pepys was a writer. T / F
4 Some people threw their things into the river. T / F
5 The fire stopped on Wednesday. T / F
6 About 80% of the people in London died. T / F
7 Christopher Wren designed the new St Paul's Cathedral. T / F
8 'The Monument' is in St Paul's Cathedral. T / F

Listening

39 **3 Listen to three teenagers. Write what they like about London under their names.**

music
the Underground
food from all over the world

....

40 **4 Listen again and answer the questions.**

1 How long has Cindy lived in London? ....
2 What does Cindy say about shops near her house? ....
3 What does Anthony think are bad things about London? ....
4 What does Julie like doing on the underground train? ....
5 What did Julie find last week? ....

A Song 4 U Waterloo sunset

41 **5 Listen and sing.**

Did you know...?

Waterloo is an old part of London. Waterloo Bridge is a bridge over the Thames, built between 1811 and 1817. It's about 750 metres long. Waterloo Station is a major railway station.

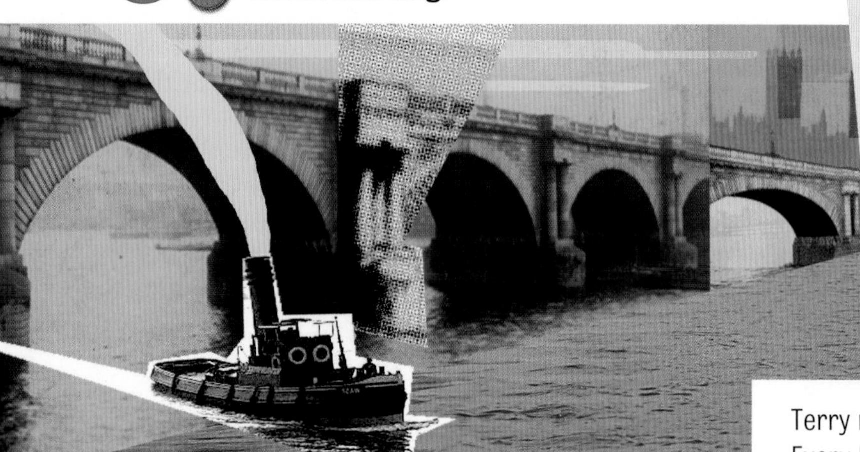

river
cross
friends
night
home
busy
at
paradise

Dirty old [1].......................... , must you keep rolling
Flowing into the night?
People so [2].......................... , makes me feel dizzy
Taxi light shines so bright.
But I don't need no [3].......................... .
As long as I gaze on Waterloo sunset
I am in paradise.

Chorus
Every day I look [4].......................... the world from my window,
But chilly, chilly is the evening time,
Waterloo sunset's fine.

Terry meets Julie, Waterloo station
Every Friday [5].......................... .
But I am so lazy, don't want to wander
I stay at [6].......................... at night.
But I don't feel afraid,
As long as I gaze on Waterloo sunset
I am in paradise.

Millions of people swarming like flies round
Waterloo Underground,
But Terry and Julie [7].......................... over the river
Where they feel safe and sound.
And they don't need no friends,
As long as they gaze on Waterloo sunset,
They are in [8].......................... .
Waterloo sunset's fine.

Writing for your Portfolio

6 **Read the letter. Then write a short letter to an English-speaking friend.**

THE SHERIDAN HOTEL
1400 88TH AVENUE
QUEENS VILLAGE
NY 16211-1000

12/8/06

Hi Sam,

Here I am in New York! It's a fantastic city.
We're in a nice hotel and the weather's good too.
Yesterday we went to The Empire State Building – I loved it,
the ride to the top was brilliant and the view was really cool!
Today we had lunch at the Hard Rock Café and tomorrow
we're going to Central Park – there's a concert there. We've got
another three days here and I'm going to have a lot more fun!
I want to see a show on Broadway!
Do you know what the best thing here is? Bagels with cream
cheese for breakfast! I love them.

See you soon!
Love, Jeanie

7 **Work with a partner. Discuss what you like about the place you live.**

The History of London

Key words

invaded	tribes	blow up	settlement
port	battle	beheaded	civil war
ruled	dockyards	monarchy	

1 **Read the text. Write down three interesting facts about London. Compare with a partner.**

London is Britain's biggest and the world's ninth largest city. 5,000 years ago, people already lived where London is today, but there were forests and marshes.

Roman London

The Romans invaded England in 43 AD. They sailed up the river Thames, and looked for a place where they could build a settlement. They chose a place where the river became narrower, and built a bridge over the river. They called the place Londinium, and the bridge was exactly where London Bridge is today. The Romans soon built a port, and Londinium became the capital of Roman Britain. Between 12,000 and 20,000 people lived in Londinium. The River Thames, which is only 100 metres wide today, was 300 metres wide! The Romans ruled Britain until 410.

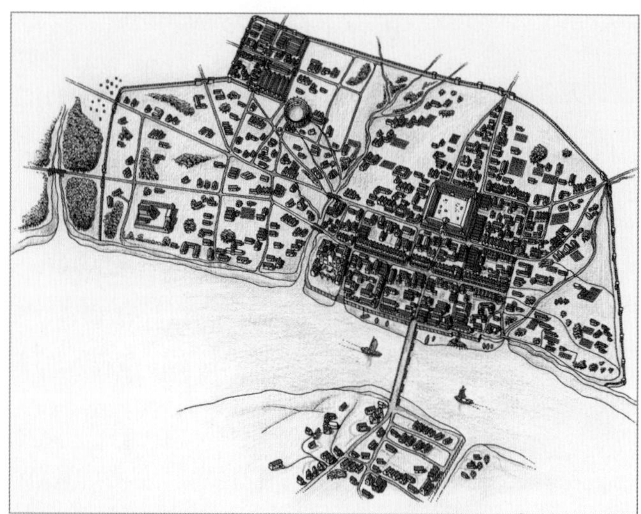

London under the Anglo-Saxons and the Vikings

Later, in the 5th century, Germanic tribes called the Anglo-Saxons settled in Britain. In the 9th century, the Danish Vikings arrived. They burnt large parts of London. Alfred the Great, the Saxon king, defeated the Vikings in 878. The two peoples divided the country between them. The Anglo-Saxons took the South and the West, and the Vikings took the East of Britain, including London. But in 886, Alfred's men took London. In 1016, the Vikings attacked London again, but the Saxons won the battle.

London in the Middle Ages

In 1066, the Normans invaded from France. They defeated the Anglo-Saxons and William I (William the Conqueror) took control. He began to build the Tower of London, and the city grew up within the Roman walls. Soon there were so many people in London that there was very little space for the people. Many of the streets were dirt streets, and people threw rubbish out of the windows onto the streets below. London was a crowded and smelly city!

Tudor London

There were about 200,000 people living in London by 1600. Most of London, as we know it today, was still fields. The Tudor kings built a lot of palaces in London and the area around. They also made big deer parks so that they could go hunting.
The river Thames was very important in Tudor times. They built dockyards and sent ships to explore the world – the Americas and India, for example.
The first theatres were built in London during this time. The most famous is of course The Globe, where Shakespeare's plays were performed. In 1613, a fire destroyed the original theatre. In the 1990s a new Globe Theatre was built, as close to the original as possible.

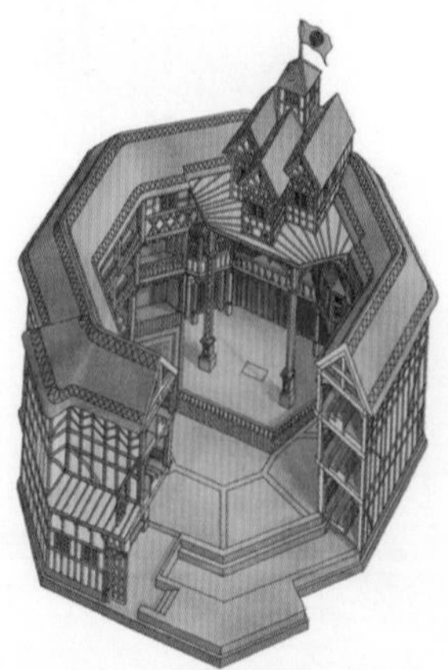

The Globe Theatre in the time of Shakespeare.

The Globe Theatre Today, re-built in the 1990s.

Stuart London

The first Stuart king after the Tudors was King James I from Scotland. In 1603, Guy Fawkes and a group of men tried to blow up the king and the Houses of Parliament. But the men were arrested.

In 1625 Charles II came to the throne. He opened Hyde Park to the people. Difficult times followed. In 1642 a civil war broke out between the king's people and Oliver Cromwell's people. The king lost and he was beheaded in London. Britain became the Commonwealth of people, a republic. In 1660, the monarchy was returned.

Mini-project My capital city

2 **Write a project about the history of your capital city. Use the example of London above as a model. Choose two different periods in your country's history. Write a short text about each one. You could include:**

- How many people lived there.
- Who the ruler of the country was.
- Any historic events that took place at the time.
- What life was like for the citizens of the city.
- Pictures to illustrate the text.

You could present the information in the form of a diary. Imagine that you are someone living in the city at each of the times you have chosen.

UNIT 6 Young people today

In this unit

You learn
- present simple passive
- *make* and *let*
- words for jobs

and then you can
- talk about ambition
- say where things are done
- say what people let you do

1 **Read the text and answer the questions.**

We built this igloo.
They are only around in the summer.
Canada's really beautiful.
My snow mobile – cool!

Hi! my name's Curtis. I live near Whitehorse, Canada, a town with a population of about 20,000. Both my parents work. My dad's a Mountie, a policeman with the Royal Canadian Mounted Police and my mother's a dentist.

In winter it's very cold in Whitehorse and there's a lot of snow. I love the winter. I have great fun riding on my snow mobile. I've got a really cool one, it's a Ski-Doo and it's made in Canada. But I'm not allowed to drive too far into the woods. My mum thinks I'll get lost out there. Last year Dad helped me and my friend Charlie to build an igloo on the frozen Yukon river. The best thing was that our parents let us spend a night in the igloo. We weren't afraid because the grizzly bears aren't around in the winter – they're all hibernating. But I think our parents were worried, because they picked us up very early in the morning.
When it snows a lot my dad makes me clear the snow away in front of the house and the garage. I don't have to do any housework, but my mum makes me keep my bedroom tidy.
My room's quite big. I have a PC there, a stereo and my own television. My parents let me watch TV until 9.30. After that I have to turn it off. There's one other thing they don't let me do – listen to my stereo at full volume when they are at home. They say my music gives them a headache!

2 Answer the questions.

1 What do Curtis' parents do?
2 Why isn't Curtis allowed to go too far into the woods?
3 Why weren't Curtis and Charlie scared of the grizzly bears?
4 What does Curtis have to do when it snows a lot?
5 What has he got in his bedroom?

Get talking Saying where things are done

42 3 Listen and match the pictures with the countries.

1 Switzerland
2 Germany
3 Brazil, Portugal
4 Italy, France
5 USA
6 Indonesia, Africa, India
7 Japan
8 South America
9 China

A 

B 

C 

D 

E 

F 

G 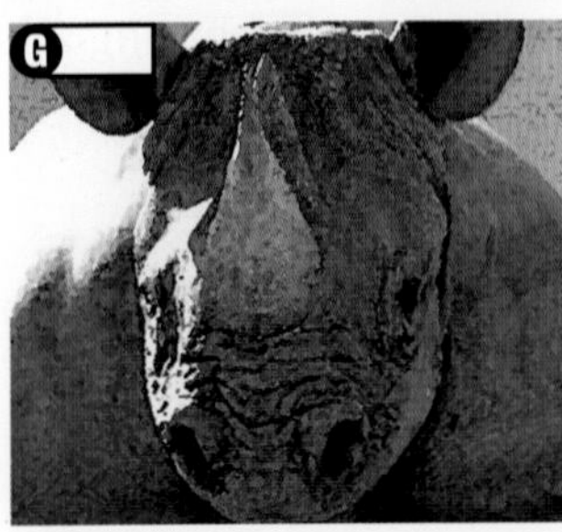

H 

I 

4 Cover up Exercise 3. Ask and answer questions with a partner.

Where is	Portuguese German the yen the yuan	spoken? used?
Where are	porsches Hollywood films swatches	made?
	truffles rhinos lamas	found?

Language Focus

Vocabulary Jobs

43 **1 Match the words and the pictures. Listen and check.**

1 writer
2 mechanic
3 nurse
4 sales assistant
5 police officer
6 computer programmer
7 waiter
8 electrician
9 doctor
10 dentist

2 What is important to you in a job? Put these things in order. (1 = most important, 10 = least important).

- ☐ working outdoors
- ☐ being creative
- ☐ helping people
- ☐ fixing things
- ☐ being independent
- ☐ being with people
- ☐ wearing a uniform
- ☐ earning a good salary
- ☐ working with young people
- ☐ having a lot of responsibility

Sounds right /i/ vs. /iː/

44 **3 Listen and repeat.**

be it eat is easy live leave give teach Portuguese

1 It isn't easy to live here.
2 Eat it quickly, please.
3 He's going to live in Italy.
4 Give it to him when you leave.
5 She wants to live in Brazil and teach Portuguese.

Get talking Talking about ambition

4 Work with a partner. Discuss what you want to be and why.

A What do you want to be?
B A teacher.
A Why?
B Because I like working with children and helping others. What about you?

Grammar

Present simple passive

1 **Look at the text on page 54 and complete the examples.**

It's a Ski-Doo and it' [1]........ [2]................... in Canada.
I [3]....... [4]................... .... to drive too far into the woods.

2 **Complete the table.**

Positive
Portuguese [1]................... **spoken** in Brazil and in Portugal. Watches [2]................... **made** in Switzerland.
Negative
Spanish [3]................... **spoken** in the UK. These cassette players [4]................... **produced** any more.
Questions and short answers
[5]................... this watch **made** in China? - **Yes, it is. / No, it isn't.** [6]................... those watches **made** in Switzerland? - **Yes, they are. / No, they aren't.**

We use the passive when we talk about actions and when it is not clear or important who the action is carried out by. You can add *by* + object to specify who the action is carried out by.

3 **Read the sentences then circle A (Active) or P (Passive) for each one.**

1 Rugby is played in many countries. A/P
2 This watch is not made any more. A/P
3 They play rugby in many countries. A/P
4 They don't make this watch any more. A/P

4 **Complete the sentences with the Present simple passive of the verbs on the right.**

1 Some new songs are only ...*sold*.... on the web.
2 Music .... illegally every day from the Internet.
3 In Africa, more than 1,000 languages ....
4 In some countries, insects .... for food.
5 Chocolate .... with cocoa beans.
6 The dollar .... in the USA.

speak
download
use
~~sell~~
eat
make

5 **Reorder the words to make questions in the Present simple passive. Then write short answers.**

1 Portuguese / spoken / in India / is? **A:** *Is Portuguese spoken in India* ? **B:** *No, it isn't*
2 olive oil / is / used / in Italy? **A:** ....? **B:** ....
3 are/ in Britain/ Mercedes cars / produced? **A:** ....? **B:** ....
4 allowed / are / to / you / drive / on the right / in England **A:** ....? **B:** ....

make and *let*

6 **Circle the correct word then check with the text on page 54.**

Our parents [1]*made / let* us spend a night in the igloo. My dad [2]*makes / lets* me clear the snow away. My mum [3]*makes / lets* me keep my bedroom tidy. My parents [4]*make / let* me watch TV until 9.30.

Now look at the question and negative form.

Do your parents make/ let you stay out late? Yes, they do. / No, they don't.

7 **Complete the rules with *make* or *let*.**

To say that someone is allowed to do something use [1]........................ + object + verb
To say that someone has to do something use [2]........................ + object + verb

8 **Complete the sentences with *make / makes / made* or *let / lets*.**

1 Yesterday my biology teacher ....made..... me stay on after the lesson for half an hour.
2 My dad often .... me do the shopping for him.
3 When I get good marks, my mum .... me use her computer.
4 I hope Ms Simmons doesn't .... us study all those words.
5 My friend didn't .... me use his iPod yesterday.
6 Last week our English teacher .... us watch a great DVD.

Get talking Saying what people let you do

45 **9** **Listen and match the phrases with the pictures.**

1 talk on the mobile phone for hours
2 smoke cigarettes
3 dye your hair
4 buy your own clothes
5 have parties at your house
6 watch TV after nine
7 ride your scooter without a helmet
8 go to discos

10 **Work in pairs. Ask and answer questions about John and Angela.**

A Do John's parents let him ride his scooter without a helmet?

B Yes, they do. / No, they don't.

Skills

Reading

1 **Read the text from a youth magazine and match the interviewer's questions with the girl's answers.**

A And where do you and your friends hang out?
B Can you tell me a little about your family?
C Do you live in a flat or a house?
D What languages do you speak, Milase?

YOUNG PEOPLE TODAY

Interviewer: 1 ☐

Milase: At home we speak KwaZulu, but at school we speak English most of the time because all our subjects are taught in English. When my parents were children, they weren't allowed to speak KwaZulu at school. That was in the time of apartheid.

Interviewer: 2 ☐

Milase: Well, my father's a waiter in a hotel and my mother's a saleswoman. I have three brothers who are six, eight and eleven.

Interviewer: 3 ☐

Milase: We live in a small house. We have a small garden and we've put big rocks around it as a fence.

Interviewer: 4 ☐

Milase: There is not much to do here, but there is a youth club next to the church. That's where I go on Saturdays and Sundays. But my parents don't let me go out when it's dark – they say it's too dangerous.

Interviewer: Thank you for the interview, Milase.

Milase: That's alright.

Did you know?

Apartheid: From 1948 – 1994 black and white people in South Africa were not allowed to be together.

2 **Match the sentence halves.**

1 Milase speaks
2 Milase's mother
3 Milase is not allowed to
4 Milase goes to a youth club
5 There are lots of dangerous people

a works in a shop.
b on Saturdays and Sundays.
c two languages.
d go out when it's dark.
e in the area where Milase lives.

Listening

46 **3** **Listen to Diego's story and circle T (True), or F (False) for the sentences below.**

1 When Diego was fourteen, he went to Mexico for the first time. T / F
2 Diego and his dad crossed the border to work on a farm. T / F
3 When he crossed the border, he had to hide under the seat of a car. T / F
4 Diego was not allowed to watch TV on the farm. T / F
5 Diego likes it in the USA. T / F
6 Now Diego's family lives in the USA. T / F

Speaking

4 **Work in pairs. Talk about some of the things your parents make and let you do.**

A My dad makes me do my homework before I watch TV.
B My mum lets me cook.

Writing for your Portfolio

5 **Read Maria's text about her family. Tick the four things she writes about.**

There are four of us in our family: my mum, my dad, my brother and me. My brother is 19 – he's an electrician. My father's 42 and he's a police officer, and my mother is 40 and she's a nurse.
We live in a small house with a garden. Our house has got three bedrooms, so my brother and I have our own rooms.
When I go out during the week, I have to be home by nine o'clock. When I go to a party at the weekends, I have to be back by midnight. I also have to keep my room tidy.

1 coming home ☐
2 physical descriptions ☐
3 where other people live ☐
4 who we all are (Dad, Mum, Sandro, me) ☐
5 the house / our rooms ☐
6 ages / jobs ☐

6 **Write a short text about your own family. First, write a list of things you want to include. Use the ideas from 5 to help you. Plan your text and then write it.**

Check your progress Units 5 and 6

1 Complete the sentences.

1 You can see shows at the t _ _ _ _ _ _ _ .
2 There is an exhibition at the m _ _ _ _ _ .
3 There is a c _ _ _ _ _ _ in the park tonight.
4 There is a parade in front of the c _ _ _ _ _ .
5 We bought some fruit at the m _ _ _ _ _ .
6 You can buy everything in a m _ _ _ s _ _ _ _.
7 There are a lot of fish in the a _ _ _ _ _ _ _

7

2 Complete the sentences. Use the Passive.

1 Fiat cars .... (make) in Turin.
2 .... baseball .... (play) in America?
3 Portuguese .... (speak) in Brazil.
4 These cars ....(not/produce) any more.
5 .... CDs .... (sell) on the Net?

5

3 Complete the dialogues. Use question tags.

A You're the boy who lives at number 34.
[1]........................?
B Yes, I am. You lived at number 12,
[2]..................................?
A Yes, we moved last year.
B You were at my school, [3]........................?
A Yes, but I go to a different school now.

A This maths homework is easy, [4]......................?
B No, it's not. You will help me, [5]........................?

A He hasn't got a new scooter, [6]........................?
B Yes, he has. He bought it yesterday.

A They are English, [7]........................?
B No, I think they're American. They were born in the USA, [8]........................?

8

4 Complete the sentences with a relative pronoun.

1 That's the car .... he bought.
2 He's the man .... taught us last year.
3 That's the book .... I'm going to buy tomorrow.
4 Fiat is a company .... makes cars.
5 She's the girl .... won the competition.

5

5 Complete the sentences with the correct job.

1 He fixes lights. He's an e _ _ _ _ _ _ _ _ _ _ .
2 She helps people who are sick.
She's a n _ _ _ _ .
3 He fixes people's teeth. He's a d _ _ _ _ _ _ .
4 He works in a garage. He's a m _ _ _ _ _ _ _ .
5 His books are famous. He's a w _ _ _ _ _ .
6 He works in a café. He's a w _ _ _ _ _ .
7 He works with computers.
He's a c _ _ _ _ _ _ _ p _ _ _ _ _ _ _ _ _ _ .
8 She sells things. She's a s _ _ _ _ w _ _ _ _ .
9 He works in a hospital. He's a d _ _ _ _ _ .
10 He helps people. He's a p _ _ _ _ _ _ _ _ .

10

6 Write the questions.

1 ....
Yes, we've got tickets for the 9 pm show.
2 ....
The film is 2 hours long.
3 ....
Yes, the supermarket is open on Sundays.
4 ....
I want to to be a teacher.
5 ....
A student ticket is £3.50.

10

7 Complete the text with the correct form of *make* or *let*.

Mark's parents [1]............... him stay up late at weekends but in the week they [2]............ him go to bed early. Last week, they [3]............ him go to bed at 9 pm every evening because he had exams. At the weekend, his mother usually [4]............... him tidy his room but then she [5]............... him use their car to go and see friends.

5

TOTAL 50

My progress so far is ...

brilliant! ☐ quite good. ☐ not great. ☐

Learn MORE about Culture

English Around the World

1 Read about world Englishes and answer the questions.

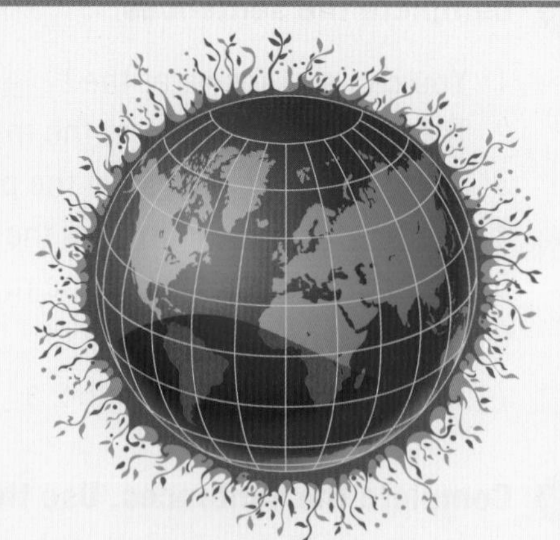

English is spoken as a native language by about 375 million people around the world. Another 750 million people speak it as a foreign language. There are now more non-native speakers of English than there are native speakers. There are more Chinese children studying English than there are British children.

The new English speakers are changing the language and new Englishes are developing around the world. There is Englog, the English spoken in the Philippines, and Japlish in Japan. There is Italglish which is spoken by the Italian immigrant population in America. There is Chinglish, Russlish, Spanglish and Hinglish. For example, *Hungry kya?* meaning *Are you hungry?* appeared on an advertisement for *Domino's* pizzas in India. Each nationality adds new words and expressions to the language and pronounces and uses it in their own way. And why are people so keen to learn English? The world needs a common language to communicate in. Today it is English but who knows – maybe tomorrow it will be Chinese, Bengali or Malay.

1 How many people speak English as a foreign language?
2 Who speaks Italglish?
3 What does *Hungry kya?* mean?
4 Which nationalities do you think speak Chinglish, Russlish, Spanglish and Hindlish?

47 **2 Look at these signs in English and another language. Which other language do you think it is? Listen and check. Then complete the summary below.**

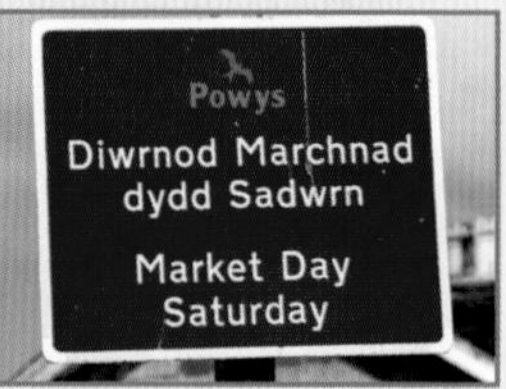

Children in Wales have to learn Welsh between the ages of [1]............ and [2]............ Welsh is used on [3]............ and in job advertisements. You can study at [4]............ in Wales in English or Welsh. Now, you can also watch [5]............ in Welsh. A big advantage of speaking Welsh is that you can always have a private [6]............ as very few people understand Welsh.

3 

Discuss the questions below with a partner.

When do you use English?
Have you seen any strange signs, advertisements or menu translations using English and another language?

There is an area in London in Clerkenwell, which is known as Little Italy. It has been the centre of the Italian community in Britain since the 19th century.

And now you can watch *The School Magazine!*

Burundi boy

Children's Express reporter Nestor Sayo left war-torn Burundi in 1995. Now, he says, he's making the most of his new life in the UK.

Even though I've spent most of my life in England, I still think lots about Burundi in Africa, because it's where I was born.

A lot of people think that I've forgotten about Burundi because I was only four years old when I left. But I always tell them, there are things I'll always remember.

Burundi was once a peaceful place but it turned into a battlefield - that's why we left.

I was very happy before war broke out between the Tutsi and Hutu people. I was part of a very big family with lots of aunts, uncles and cousins. But many of them, children and grown-ups, were killed in the fighting.

When my mother and I left Burundi, we travelled on a bus for 8 hours to Uganda. It was so tiring and all we had to eat was two slices of bread. We were only in Uganda for a short time before moving onto Kenya, where we stayed for a few months.

One day my mother took me to the airport and told me we were going to catch a plane. I didn't even know which country we'd end up in. We landed and I found out we were in England.

It was December, right in the middle of winter. Coming from Africa I was freezing.

The first few weeks of my new life in England were spent in a hotel, somewhere outside London, in a town I don't even know the name of. Then we got sent to a hotel for refugee families in Finsbury Park, in London.

There were lots of people at the hotel from all over the world – people from China, India, Brazil and Africa.

I couldn't speak English but it didn't take me long to pick up things like "Hello". My Mum knew only three words – "No English" and "Sorry".

I liked the hotel in Finsbury Park because there were other children to play with and they shared their toys with me.

I was also happy that my mum met another woman from Burundi because it meant she had someone to talk to in our own language and she wouldn't be lonely.

In some ways, I think of London as being "home". I've made loads of friends here and I'm just as proud to support the England football team as anyone born here.

Sometimes I miss Burundi but some of my family are still living there. I know I'll go back and visit them. Maybe one day I'll even be able to buy a house there.

For MORE! Go to www.cambridge.org/elt/more and do a quiz on this text.

UNIT 7 I didn't use to like them

In this unit

You learn

- words for music *used to*
- *so do I/ neither do I*

and then you can

- talk about what you used to do
- agree and disagree

Read and listen to the dialogue.

Claire Listen to that! What a laugh! I used to like them.

Karen Who is it? I can't even remember them.

Rick Neither can I, and I had to listen to all of Claire's weird CDs when I was younger!

Claire It's *Ha Ha* by All Saints.

Karen Oh, my goodness! Yes, it is! I remember it now.

Oliver So do I. You used to dance to this all the time.

Claire Don't remind me! So, what else have we got here?

Oliver U2 - I didn't use to like them, but now I'm quite a big fan. In fact, I've got most of their CDs. So, what are you into right now, Rick?

Rick Post-punk stuff – a lot of old music, too. I've just borrowed my brother's collection of Rage Against the Machine. It's weird, but I like it. He used to spend all his pocket money on CDs so he's got a massive collection.

Claire I used to do that but now I've started a Tolkien collection. There's loads of things you can buy.

Karen Have you got the 12-disk set of *Lord of the Rings*?

Claire Of course!

2 **Answer the questions.**

1 Who used to like All Saints?
2 Who is a U2 fan?
3 What kind of music does Rick like at the moment?
4 What did Rick's brother use to do with all his pocket money?
5 What kind of collection has Claire got?
6 Has she always collected these things?

Get talking Talking about what you used to do

49 **3** **Listen and repeat.**

Interviewer Which TV series did you use to watch when you were 10?
Girl I used to watch *Charmed*!

Interviewer What did you use to like when you were younger?
Boy I used to like roller-skating.

50 **4** **Match the questions and answers. Then listen and check.**

Questions

1 Dad, what music did you listen to when you were young?
2 Gran, did you watch a lot of TV when you were a girl?
3 How did you use to spend your Saturdays, mum?
4 Did you use to read a lot, John?
5 What was your favourite TV series, Natasha?

Answers

a Not really – I didn't like TV. I used to read.
b When I was small, I used to watch *Buffy*!!
c I used to like the Beatles a lot.
d No – I used to go to the cinema a lot.
e I used to go dancing on Saturdays!

5 **Work in pairs. Ask each other questions about what you used to do when you were younger.**

A What did you use to watch when you were younger?

B I used to watch cartoons all the time!

Language Focus

Vocabulary Music

1 Number the musical styles. (1 = your favourite, 13 = your least favourite).

☐ Dance

☐ Rap

☐ Folk

☐ Indie

☐ Hip-hop

☐ Opera

☐ Pop

☐ Jazz

☐ Country

☐ Blues

☐ Rock

☐ Heavy metal

☐ Classical

Get talking Agreeing and disagreeing

51 **2 Complete the dialogue with the phrases from the left. Listen and check.**

Oh, I do
Neither do I
So do I

Richard Do you like dance music?
Susan No, I don't.
Richard [1] .... , but my sister does. She's got hundreds of dance CDs.
Susan So what do you like?
Richard Well, classic punk like The Jam.
Susan [2] .... Have you got any Green Day CDs too?
Richard Yes, but I don't like them that much.
Susan [3] .... I really do.

3 Work with a partner. Talk about the music you like or dislike.

A What music do you like? / don't you like?
B I like / don't like ....
A So do I / Neither do I / Oh, I don't!

Grammar

used to

1 Complete the sentences then check with the dialogue on page 64.

You [1] .... to this all the time.
He [2] .... all his pocket money on CDs, so he's got a massive collection.
I [3] .... them, but now I'm quite a big fan.

We use *used to / didn't use to* (+ verb) to talk about past habits.
The question (*Did you use to ...?*) is almost never used.

2 Put the words in the correct order.

1 live / there / I / to / used ......I used to live there.......
2 to my school / used / go / She / to ....
3 the USA / to / We / live / used / in ....
4 to / vegetables / didn't / eat / I / use ....
5 have / didn't / to / I / use / my own bedroom ....
6 rock / didn't / like / My father / to / use / music ....

3 Complete with one of the phrases on the right.

used to eat
didn't use to eat
used to play
didn't use to play
used to go
didn't use to go
used to speak
~~didn't use to speak~~

1 I ...didn't use to speak... English, but now I can say some things.
2 Steve .... the guitar at all, but now he plays very well.
3 My brother hates pizza, but when he was younger he .... it every day.
4 My mother .... Spanish, but now she's forgotten it.
5 We never go to the cinema these days, but we .... every weekend.
6 My parents .... on holiday, but now they go to France every year.
7 My favourite player is Ronaldo – he .... for Inter Milan.
8 I .... spinach, but now I really love it!

4 Complete with *used to* or *didn't use to* and a verb from the box.

~~speak~~	eat	wear	live	be	do

1 My father ..used to speak.. a bit of Japanese, but now he's forgotten it all.
2 My sister .... only white clothes, but now she likes lots of different colours.
3 My brother .... a very nervous person, but he isn't any more.
4 I .... any exercise, but now I run 4 times a week.
5 I .... vegetables, but now I eat them all the time.
6 We .... in a really small flat, but now we've got a big house.

so do I / neither do I

5 **Complete the examples then check with the dialogue on page 64.**

Karen I remember it now.
Oliver [1] .... You used to dance to this all the time.
Karen I can't even remember them.
Rick [2] ...., and I had to listen to them when I was younger.

We use these phrases to agree with what another person says.
Present Simple
If the other person says something positive, use: *So do I.*
If the other person says something negative, use: *Neither do I*
Other verbs
'**I'm** tired.' '**So am I**.' 'I **can't** sing.' '**Neither can I**.' 'I arrived late.' '**So did I**.'

6 **Complete the dialogue with these phrases.**

So do I.	So did I.	~~So can I.~~	So have I.
Neither do I.	Neither did I.	Neither can I.	Neither have I.

1 **A** Look! I can walk on my hands!
B So can I!
2 **A** This homework's hard – I can't do it.
B ....
3 **A** I've got a new bike.
B ....
4 **A** I always go to the cinema on Fridays.
B ....
5 **A** We enjoyed ourselves at the party.
B ....
6 **A** I've never been to France.
B ....
7 **A** I didn't go out last night.
B ....
8 **A** My sister doesn't like rap.
B ....

7 **Complete the replies.**

1 I love chocolate! So do I.
2 My brother's got an iPod. ....
3 I went to Greece last year. ....
4 I don't know the answer. ....
5 I'm sorry, I can't go out tonight. ....
6 She didn't pass the test. ....
7 Mary can sing hip-hop. ....

8 **Find sentences you agree with. Write *So ... I* or *Neither ... I.* Compare your answers with a partner.**

1 I'm thirteen. ....
2 I'm not interested in sport. ....
3 I love football. ....
4 I watched television last night. ....
5 I read magazines a lot. ....
6 I can't speak Spanish. ....
7 I didn't enjoy myself last night. ....
8 I can walk on my hands. ....
9 I think hip-hop is great. ....
10 I was at school yesterday. ....
11 I wasn't at home on Sunday. ....
12 I haven't been to England. ....

Skills

Reading

 52  **Read and listen. Match the photos to the paragraphs.**

THE FAB FOUR

John Lennon, Paul McCartney, George Harrison and Ringo Starr – together they were the Beatles, the greatest band the world has ever seen. Here are eight of the most important events in their history.

Lennon and McCartney meet

On July 6th 1957 fifteen-year-old Paul McCartney first met John Lennon in Liverpool. John Lennon was on stage with his band *The Quarry Men*. Later in the evening Paul played piano with the band. They thought he was so good that they asked him to join them.

The Beatles move to Germany 1 ☐

In August 1960 the Beatles went to Germany, where they played at Hamburg's Star Club until December 1st. The band was made up of John Lennon (rhythm guitar/vocals), Paul McCartney (rhythm/vocals), George Harrison (lead guitar/vocals), and two other musicians on the bass and the drums.

The early hits 2 ☐

In the summer of 1962, a new drummer, Ringo Starr, joined John, Paul and George. On October 11th 1962 the Beatles made their first appearance in the UK charts with *Love Me Do.* In early 1963 their second single *Please, Please, Me* became their first number 1. The Beatles quickly followed this with another number 1 single *From Me to You* and a number 1 album, also called *Please, Please, Me.*

The Beatles invade the USA 3 ☐

On February 7th 1964, 10,000 fans were at New York's Kennedy Airport to see Pan-Am flight PA101 land. On board were Paul, John, George and Ringo. Four days later the Beatles played their first US concert in Washington DC to 8,600 screaming fans. More than 70 million Americans watched their performance on TV. On April 4th 1964 the top five singles in the US charts were *Can't Buy me Love, Twist and Shout, She Loves You, I Want to Hold your Hand*, and *Please, Please Me* – all of them Beatles songs!

Sergeant Pepper's Lonely Hearts Club Band

On June 1st 1967 the Beatles released their eighth album, *Sergeant Pepper's Lonely Hearts Club Band.* Many people think this is the greatest of all their records. The album had the famous songs *She's Leaving Home, When I'm Sixty-Four* and *Lucy in the Sky with Diamonds.* It was also famous for its cover, which showed pictures of many of the band's idols.

The last show

On January 30th 1969 the Beatles played their last concert. It was a show on the roof of their record company in London. A large group of fans watched from the street below, but there were complaints about the noise from neighbours so the police arrived and stopped the show after only 42 minutes. Just over a year later, the band broke up.

E

Liverpool Echo

Crazed gunman charged

JOHN LENNON SHOT DEAD

JOHN LENNON, of the legendary Liverpool pop group, The Beatles, was shot dead in New York to-day by a crazed gunman.

After a man police described as "a local screwball" pumped five bullets into Lennon, he yelled "I'm shot" and staggered up a few steps into the apartment building where he lived.

And as the 40-years-old superstar lay dying in the arms of his wife, Yoko Ono, his last whispered words were "Help Me," according to neighbour Carrie Rouse.

The death of John Lennon 4 ☐

On December 8th 1980, when John Lennon was outside his home in New York with his wife, Yoko Ono, a crazy fan called Mark Chapman shot him. John's death was a great shock all over the world — people now knew that the Beatles' would never play together again.

The release of *One* 5 ☐

In November 2000, a compilation of the Beatles' number 1 hits called *One* went straight to the top of the UK album charts. It was the fastest selling CD of the year and sold 320,000 in the first week. It also reached number 1 in many other countries around the world including Germany, France, Spain and Canada. It demonstrated that the Beatles were still one of the biggest and most popular bands in the world.

2 Write the questions for these answers.

1 In Liverpool in 1957. *When and where did Paul first meet John?*
2 In August 1960. ....
3 *Please, Please Me.* ....
4 10,000. ....
5 In the summer of 1962. ....
6 On the roof of their record company. ....

Listening

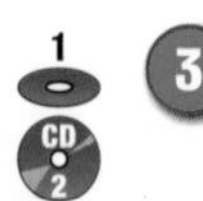

3 Paul Sacks and Sally Green are critics on the hit TV talent show *Superstar*. Listen and write the name of the person these sentences refer to (Jasmine or Dave).

1 Your voice needs a little more training. ....
2 You're not going to be our next superstar. ....
3 You look fantastic. ....
4 You gave it a try and that's what's important. ....
5 We certainly want to talk to you again. ....
6 You were out of tune. ....

Speaking

2 **4 Work in pairs. Listen to these three performers and say what you think.**

Steve

Tina

Jeff

... looks fantastic / doesn't look like a pop star.
...'s got a beautiful / terrible voice / needs (doesn't need) training.
... is an excellent singer / was out of tune / has(n't) got what it takes
... could be the next pop star / is never going to make it as a pop star / is(n't) on the way up

Writing for your Portfolio

5 Read the text and put the headings in the correct places.

Career
Full Name
Why I like her music
Born

My favourite singer

1 .... : Beyonce Giselle Knowles

2 .... : Houston, Texas, in 1981

3 .... : Beyonce began as a member of the band Destiny's Child. Their records sold millions of copies. In 2003 Beyonce released her first solo album, *Dangerously in Love.* In 2006 she starred in the films *The Pink Panther* and *Dreamgirls*

4 .... : I love Beyonce's music because she has an excellent voice, and she is a great performer. My favourite Beyonce songs are *Beautiful Liar* and *Irreplaceable.*

6 Now write a short summary about a pop star / band that you like.

Musical instruments

Key words

bamboo, binding, folk music, pear-shaped body, metallic, stringed, an opening

1 **Look at the pictures of the four musical instruments.**

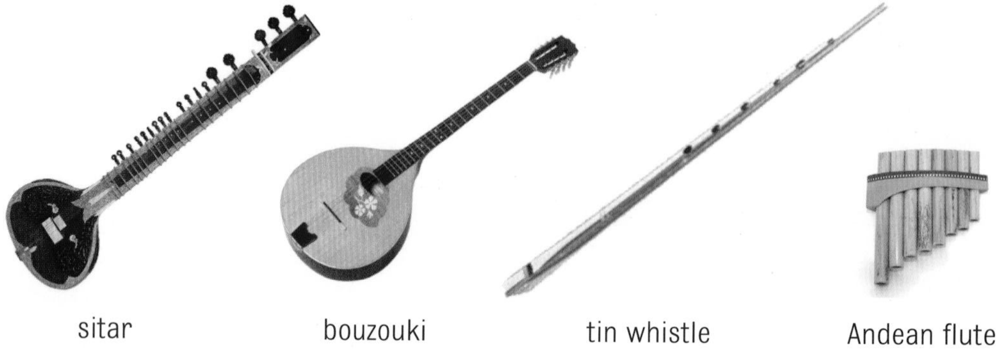

sitar   bouzouki   tin whistle   Andean flute

3 **2** **Listen. Guess which instrument you hear. Write the numbers next to the names of the instruments.**

sitar .... bouzouki .... tin whistle .... Andean flute ....

3 **Write the names of the instruments from above into the text.**

The [1]... comes from Ecuador and is made of bamboo. It has 7 notes and is very easy to play. It often has a decorative binding.
The [2]... is important in modern Greek music as well as in other Balkan folk music. It is a stringed instrument with a pear-shaped body and a very long neck. The instrument has a sharp metallic sound.
The [3]... is a simple wind instrument with six holes. It can made out of different kinds of metal. It is very popular in traditional Irish music. Many children in Ireland play it because it is cheap to buy and easy to learn.
The [4]... is probably the best-known South Asian instrument in the West. It is an Indian classical stringed instrument. It became popular in the West when The Beatles used it in many songs. It is difficult to play.

4 **4** **Folk music across the continents. The extracts you are going to hear are from Australia, Asia, North America, South America and Europe. Guess where they are from.**

I think number one is from …

I don't think so, it's from …

5 **Look at the orchestra. Label the different sections.**

a) wind b) brass c) percussion d) string

6 **Listen to the three following pieces of classical music. Which instruments can you hear?**

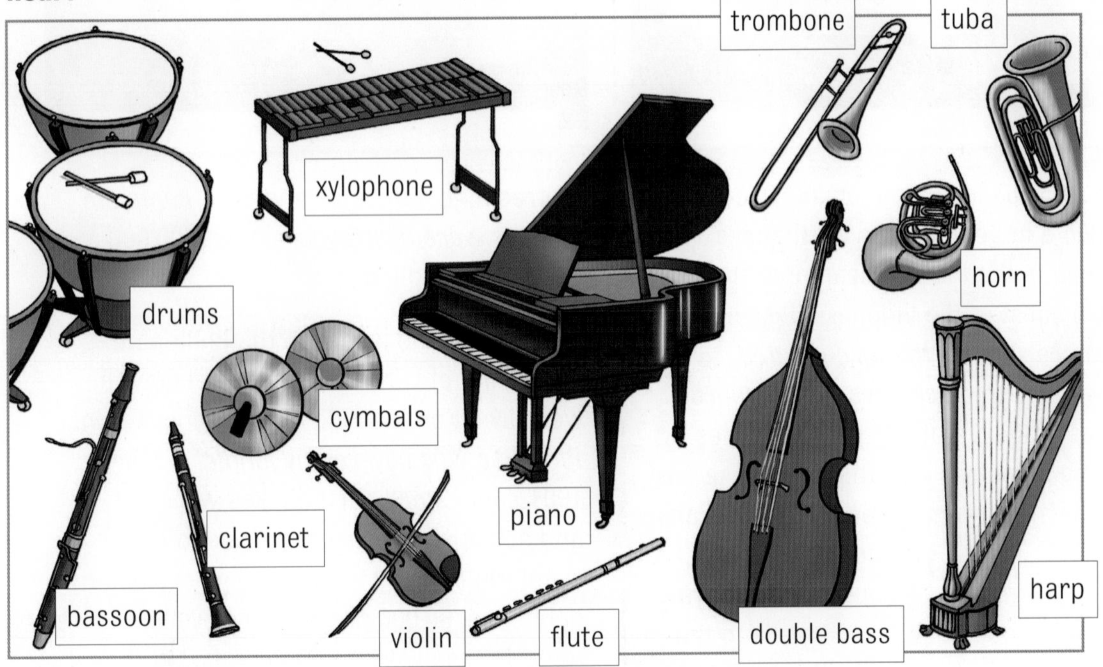

Mini-project Instruments from around the world

7 **Find out about two unusual instruments from your country. Write a short text about each one. Include a picture.**

UNIT 8 Natural disasters

1 Read the webpage. Write the sentences in italics under the pictures.

   http://www.historynews.net

Great disasters of the modern world

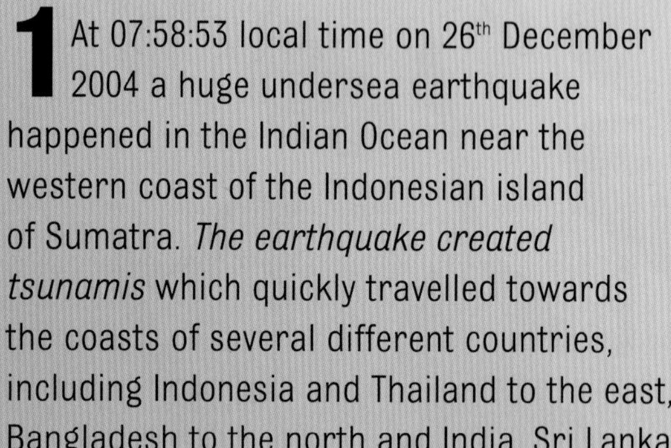

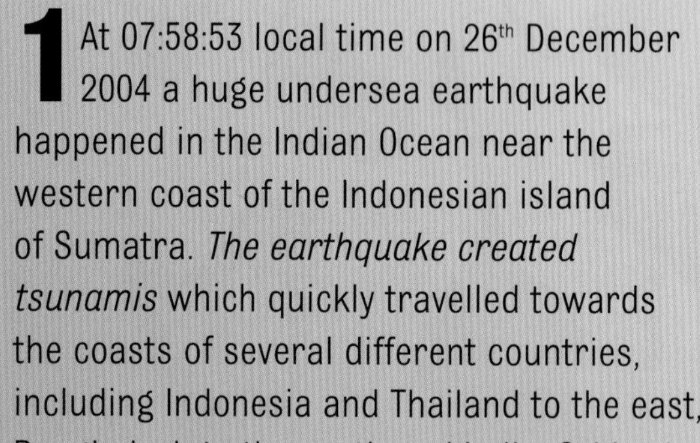

1 At 07:58:53 local time on 26th December 2004 a huge undersea earthquake happened in the Indian Ocean near the western coast of the Indonesian island of Sumatra. *The earthquake created tsunamis* which quickly travelled towards the coasts of several different countries, including Indonesia and Thailand to the east, Bangladesh to the north and India, Sri Lanka and even the African countries of Kenya and Somalia to the west. Warnings were sent but they arrived too late. Many of the coasts of these countries were hit by huge waves up to 15 metres high. Buildings and even *complete villages were destroyed.* Almost 300,000 people were killed.

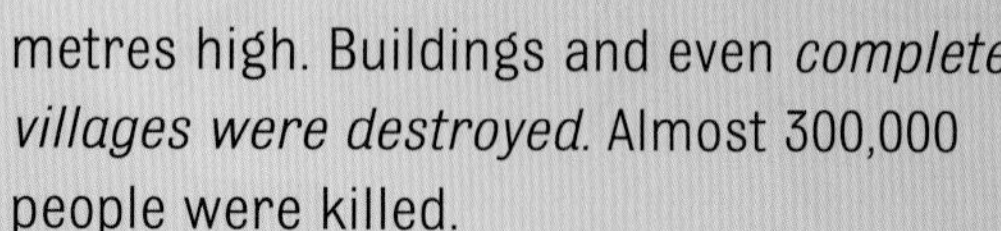

2 Most of the locals on the Philippine island of Luzon did not even know they were living on the side of a volcano. *Mount Pinatubo was covered by jungle.* In March 1991 some small earthquakes were felt and scientists warned the volcano could erupt. On June 3rd the first large explosion happened. 60,000 people were evacuated. *On June 15th the volcano finally erupted.* It sent ash and rocks 34 km into the air and the lava ran for 16 km. 300 people were killed.

In this unit

You learn

- *too/ not … enough*
- past passive
- words for catastrophes

and then you can

- express sympathy
- explain things in simpler words
- talk about where people were born

2 **Circle T (True) or F (False) for the sentences below.**

1 The Indian Ocean disaster happened in November 2004. T / F
2 Countries on four continents were affected by the Indian Ocean tsunami. T / F
3 Almost 300,000 people were killed. T / F
4 The locals on Luzon always knew that they were living in danger. T / F
5 60,000 people on the island of Luzon left their homes. T / F

Get talking Expressing sympathy

6 **3** **Listen to the conversation. Complete it with the expressions on the right.**

A 1 .... **B** Well, not really.
A 2 .... **B** It's about our dog.
A 3 .... **B** It died yesterday.
A 4 ....

Are you OK, Sandra?

What about it?

Oh, I'm so sorry to hear that.

What's the matter?

4 **Choose situations. Act out dialogues like the one above.**

next weekend / I'm not allowed to come to your birthday party

tonight / I can't come to the cinema

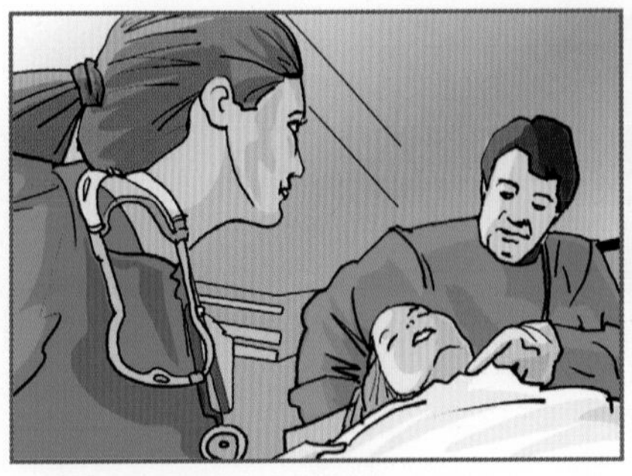
sister / was taken to hospital yesterday

best friend / had a bike accident last week

new MP3 player / I broke it this morning

maths test / I got very bad results

Language Focus

Vocabulary Catastrophes

7 **1 Match the words with their definitions. Then listen and check.**

1 ☐ a lot of water covering a place that is usually dry.
2 ☐ a long time without rain.
3 ☐ a mass of mud and earth sliding down a mountain.
4 ☐ a mountain with a large hole at the top through which lava comes out.
5 ☐ a violent wind, especially found in the West Atlantic Ocean.
6 ☐ an extremely large wave that often happens after an earthquake.
7 ☐ when masses of ice and snow fall quickly down the side of a mountain.
8 ☐ when the earth shakes so strongly that sometimes houses are destroyed.
9 ☐ when a forest starts to burn.

a an earthquake

b an avalanche

c a volcano

d a flood

e a drought

f a tsunami

g a forest fire

h a mudslide

i a hurricane

Get talking Explaining things in simpler words

2 Cover up Exercise 1. In pairs, ask and answer questions.

A What's an 'earthquake'?

B It's when the earth shakes so strongly that sometimes houses are destroyed.

B What's a 'volcano'?

A A volcano? That's a mountain with hot lava inside. The lava comes out through a hole at the top.

Grammar

too / not ... enough

Warnings were sent but they	arrived **too** late. did**n't** arrive soon **enough**.

1 **Complete the sentences with the adjectives on the right.**

good
strong
~~tall~~
tired
late

1 He's not ....tall.... enough to get the apple from the tree.
2 We're too .... to see the film. It started 15 minutes ago.
3 I'm not .... enough to be in the school football team.
4 She's too .... to do her homework now. She should go to bed.
5 You're not .... enough to lift this.

Past passive

2 **Complete the examples with words from the box then check with the text on page 74.**

were destroyed	was covered	were hit
were sent	were evacuated	were killed

Mount Pinatubo [1] .... by jungle.
Warnings [2] ....
Many of the coasts of these countries [3] .... by huge waves.
Complete villages [4] ....
Almost 300,000 people [5] ....
60,000 people [6] ....

3 **Decide if the sentences are passive or active.**

1 The hurricane destroyed thousands of homes. – *active*
2 Breakfast is served until 10 am.
3 He was paid a lot of money for the photo.
4 We're not very happy with our room.
5 The teacher was 10 minutes late for the lesson.
6 Children under 11 are not allowed into the pub.

4 **Write sentences with the Past passive. Use the words below and *by*.**

1 The email / write / Susan ..... *The email was written by Susan.*
2 The cakes / make / Fred ....
3 The race / win / an Ethiopian ....
4 The children / rescue / the police ....
5 My website / design / my sister ....
6 The pictures / paint / a famous artist ....

Sounds right 'r' sound

5 Listen and repeat. Pay attention to the 'r' sound.

water earthquake destroyed
were erupted

6 Listen and repeat the sentences.

What's the matter?
The volcano erupted.
The buildings were destroyed.

Get talking Talking about when people were born

7 Write the number of the correct word in the pictures.

1 telephone
2 light bulb
3 car
4 jeans
5 nuclear reactor
6 windscreen wipers
7 dynamite
8 signal flare
9 dishwasher

8 Write the names of the inventors under the pictures. Then discuss your answers with a partner.

A

B
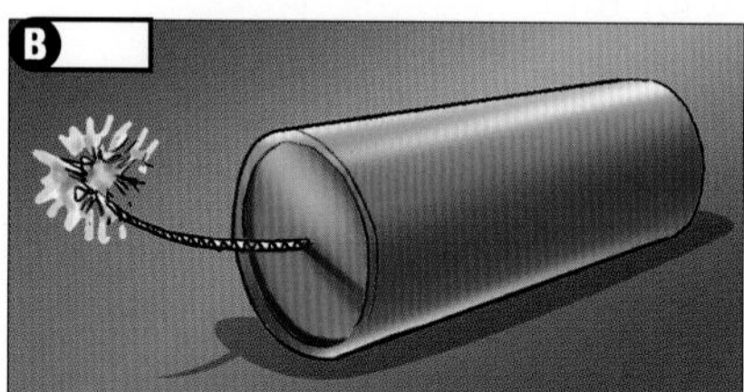

C

D

E
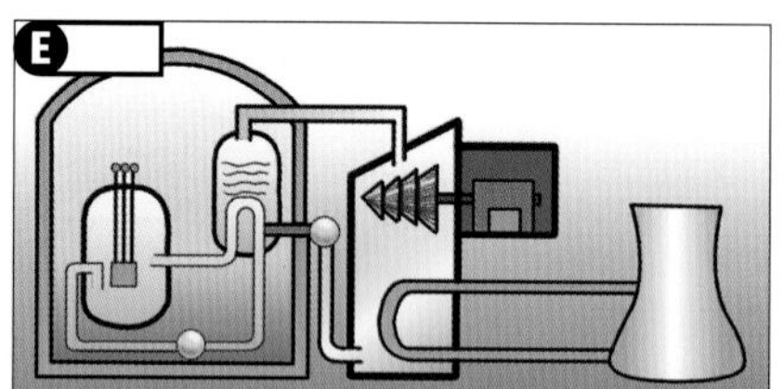

F
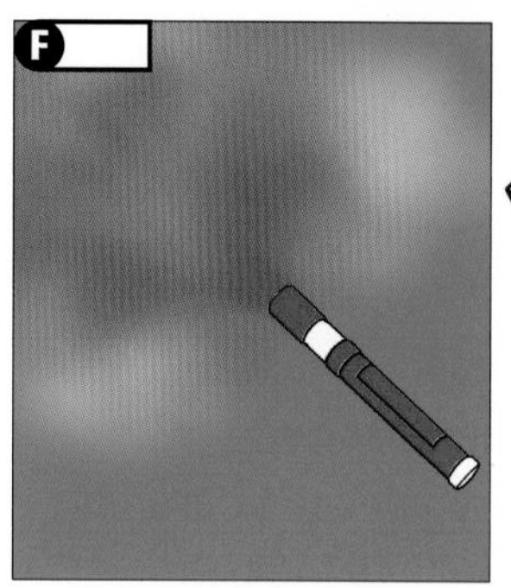

G
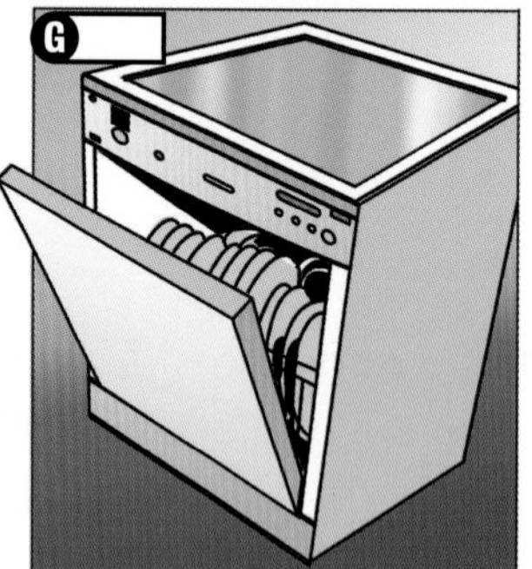

H

I
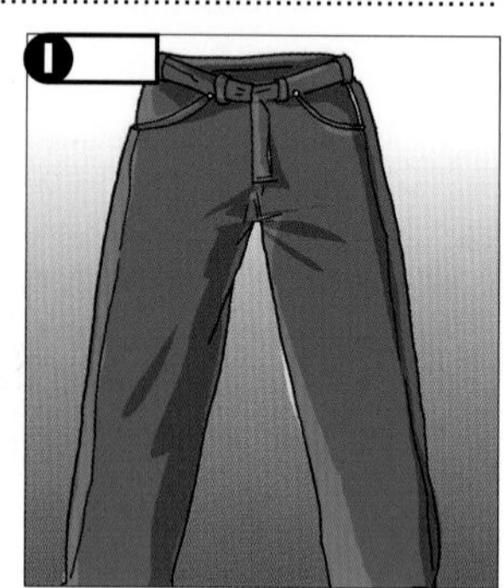

Mary Anderson *(born 1866 in Alabama, USA)*
Gottlieb Daimler *(born 1834 in Stuttgart, Germany)*
Josephine Cochrane *(born 1839 in Illinois, USA)*
Thomas Alva Edison *(born 1847 in Ohio, USA)*
Alfred Nobel *(born 1833 in Stockholm, Sweden)*
Levi Strauss *(born 1847 in Bavaria, Germany)*
Enrico Fermi *(born 1901 in Rome, Italy)*
Alexander Graham Bell *(born 1847 in Edinburgh, Scotland)*
Martha Coston *(born 1826 in Baltimore, USA)*

A I think the car was invented by Levi Strauss.

B I don't think so. I think it was invented by Gottlieb Daimler. / I think so too.

Reading

1 Read the story.

CASTAWAY!

1 Chuck's plane was flying over open sea when the storm started. The plane ran into trouble when the storm got stronger. ☐

2 Eventually it crashed, but Chuck survived and he started swimming. ☐

3 On the island, Chuck learned how to open coconuts to get the milk, and which berries were good to eat. ☐

4 After two or three weeks, he opened some of the packages that had washed ashore from the plane wreckage. ☐

5 ☐ He amused himself by drawing a face on the ball with some of the blood. He gave the ball a name, too.

I know – I'll call you 'Wilson'.

6 ☐ Wilson became Chuck's best friend – and when Chuck escaped from the island on a raft 6 months later, he took Wilson with him.

7 After three days at sea, Wilson fell off the raft, but Chuck couldn't get him back. ☐

8 The following day, several months after the plane crash, a miracle happened. ☐

2 Write the letters of the extra sentences from the story in the boxes above.

A He also learned how to catch and cook fish.
B Chuck was rescued and taken back to the USA.
C After swimming for a long time, he reached a desert island.
D The pilot couldn't control the plane.
E Chuck gave up hope and just lay on the raft.
F He was surprised to find a ball in one of them.
G There was no-one else to talk to, so Chuck talked to Wilson.
H One day, Chuck fell over and cut his arm.

Listening

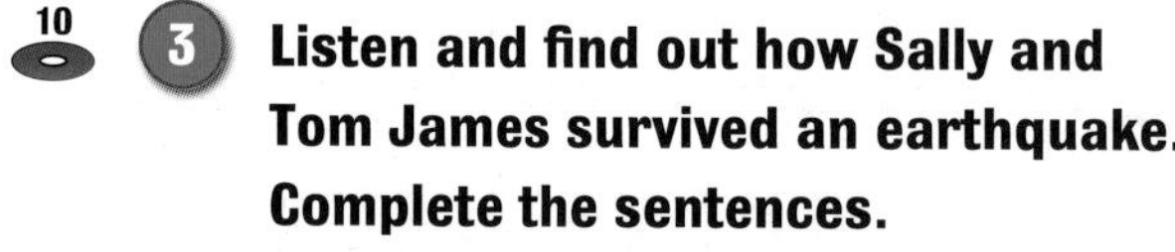

10 **3 Listen and find out how Sally and Tom James survived an earthquake. Complete the sentences.**

1 Sally was getting breakfast ready when ....
2 She looked out of the window and saw ....
3 Just before the big quake happened, she ....
4 She shouted and some men came. They ....
5 Tom was on his way ....
6 He stopped his car and ....
7 He ran as fast as he could until he ....
8 When he came back to the car, ...

Speaking

4 Imagine you are going to spend a year alone on a desert island. You are allowed to take a CD, a book, a DVD and one other thing with you. Work in pairs. Choose your items and interview each other.

A What DVD are you going to take?

B I'm going to take *Titanic* because ...

Writing for your Portfolio

5 Read Paul's story about a forest fire near his home then complete it with these words.

then ago first When after later

Two years [1]......, there was a bad forest fire near my town. At [2]......, it wasn't a problem, but [3]...... two days, the firemen said people had to leave their houses. So we put some clothes into suitcases, [4]...... we got in the car and drove to my grandparents' house. Three days [5]......, the fire stopped, and we drove back to our house. [6]...... we got there, we saw that the house was OK. We were happy to be back home again!

6 Write a story about someone who survived an earthquake. Use these verbs and the time words from Exercise 5.

to escape to rescue to crush to shake to collapse a tremor safe

Check your progress Units 7 and 8

1 Complete the words for types of music.

1 o _ _ _ _
2 f _ _ _
3 c _ _ _ _ _ _ _
4 i _ _ _ _
5 h _ _ _ _ m _ _ _ _
6 d _ _ _ _
7 b _ _ _ _

7

2 Read the descriptions and complete the words.

1 When there is no rain for a long time.
a d _ _ _ _ _ _
2 When the earth shakes.
an e _ _ _ _ _ _ _ _ _ _
3 When there is too much water.
a f _ _ _ _
4 Rocks and earth which fall down a mountain.
an a _ _ _ _ _ _ _ _ _
5 A violent wind.
a h _ _ _ _ _ _ _ _
6 A mountain with lava inside.
a v _ _ _ _ _ _

6

3 Complete the dialogue with the correct form of *used to*.

A Which school did you [1]...................... go to?
B I [2]...................... go to Mansfield School.
A I didn't [3]...................... like school but this year I'm enjoying it.
B That's good. I hope I enjoy this school too!

3

4 Rewrite the sentences using the Past simple passive.

1 The hurricane destroyed the forest.
....
2 Van Gogh painted that picture.
....
3 Mark wrote these emails.
....
4 Sarah won the money.
....
5 An Englishman built these houses.
....

10

5 Complete the sentences with *too* or *not ... enough*.

1 He is not .... (good) to play for the basketball team.
2 We are .... (late) to see the film. It started 10 minutes ago.
3 They were not .... (strong) to lift the boxes.
4 I was .... (tired) to stay up late.

4

6 Write the questions.

1 ....?
He was born in 1972.
2 ....?
Yes, I like jazz.
3 ....?
I'm sad about my dog.
4 ....?
It's when the earth shakes.
5 ....?
I'm going to take a good book on holiday.

10

7 Complete the dialogues with the correct phrase.

Yes, I do.	So do I.	Do you want
What about	I like	Neither do I.

A Do you like U2?
B [1]..
A That's good. [2]..
B [3]...................................... Green Day?
A I don't like them.
B [4]..
A [5]................................ rock music these days. In fact, I'm going to a concert tomorrow. [6]................................ to come?

6

What's the matter?	Are you OK
not really	I'm so sorry to hear that.

A [7]......................................, Sue?
B No, [8]..
A [9]..
B It's my grandmother. She's not very well.
A [10]......................................

4

TOTAL 50

My progress so far is ...

brilliant! ☐ quite good. ☐ not great. ☐

Learn MORE about Culture

Manga!

1 **Discuss the questions below then read the text and answer the questions.**

Do you read manga comics?
Do you watch manga cartoons?
Who is your favourite manga character?

Did YOU know?

The word 'manga' means comic in Japanese. Mangas are written for both adults and children. The Japanese manga industry is HUGE. It is much bigger than the comic industry in both America and France. Yearly sales of manga books and magazines are approximately 57 million dollars.

So how did manga start? Cartoon drawing began in Japan almost eight hundred years ago. Artists drew manga on temple walls. These pictures were very similar to modern manga. In 1702, Shumboko Ono, a famous artist, made a book of these pictures and added captions. Manga artists started to use stories as well as illustrations. These comic books were called *Tobae*. They were the main form of literature for Japanese society. In 1947, Tezuka Osamu, a young medical student created *New Treasure Island* which was a great success. He became the father of 'modern' manga. His most popular work is *Mighty Atom*. He also created *Astro Boy* and *Kimba the White Lion*.

Today, in Japan, manga can be found on every street corner. Manga magazines contain at least 200-400 pages of manga an issue. Hundreds of manga artists work individually or in small groups. Popular manga characters become TV cartoons or animated films which are watched all over the world.

1 Is manga an old or a new art?
2 What is *Tobae*?
3 Who became the father of modern manga?
4 How long are most Manga magazines?

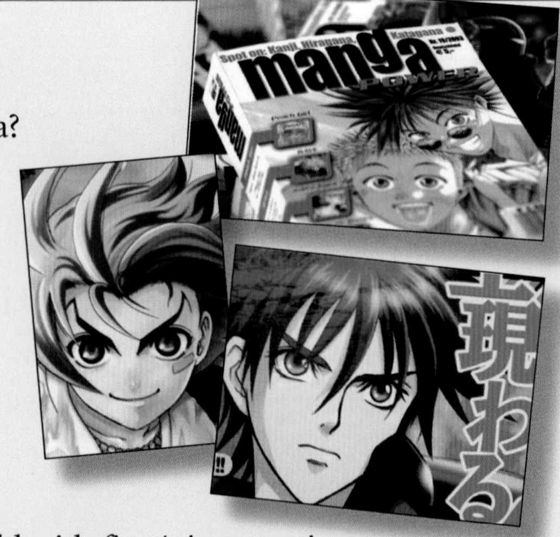

11 **2** **Listen and circle the correct word to complete the sentences below.**

1 *Naruto* comes from *a book / a magazine*.
2 *Naruto* takes place in a make-believe world with *five / six* countries.
3 Each country has a hidden *village / city* where Ninja live.
4 The name Ninja was the name of *teachers / spies* in the Samurai age.
5 Uzumaki Naruto is a *good / bad* student.
6 He has got a *ten-tailed / nine-tailed* fox inside his body.
7 He has *no / great* strength in times of danger.
8 Naruto's peers *don't possess / all possess* their own special powers.

3 

Work in pairs and design a new manga character. Write an adventure for him or her, then present it to the class.

MORE! And now you can watch *The School Magazine!* DVD

HOW TO SURVIVE

Earthquakes

Do you ever get tired of all that advice you get in teen magazines? You know, stuff like how to survive at school, how to survive your parents, how to survive exams – things like that.
Well I live in San Francisco and here we have something a bit more dangerous than parents and exams – they're called earthquakes and here's my survival guide.

HOW TO SURVIVE – Earthquakes.

Keep calm. If you are inside, first of all get down on the floor and find some cover to protect you from falling objects – a heavy table or desk, for example. Keep away from windows and objects that could fall on you.
If you are outside, move quickly away from buildings, street lights and trees. Try and find an open area.
If you are in a public building, do not rush to the door. That's what everyone else will do. Never use a lift during an earthquake.
After the quake has finished watch out for aftershocks. These are follow-up quakes. They are usually smaller than the first one but they can still cause damage. They can cause things to fall down.
When you leave your house, make sure you are wearing shoes. They will be a lot of broken glass on the ground, for sure.

So how big was that quake?

The strength of each earthquake is measured on the Richter scale. It goes from 0 to 8.9. Here's a guide to what happens at each point on the scale.

7.3 – 8.9

Total destruction;
roads break up and rocks fall.
The ground opens up.

6.2 – 7.3

People are starting to panic.
Buildings start to fall down.
Water is thrown out of rivers.

4.8 – 6.2

Now you are finding it difficult to stand up or walk.
Windows break and tiles fall off roofs.

4.3 – 4.8

If you were sleeping, you're not any more.
Dishes, doors and trees shake and rock.

0 – 4.3

Lying on your bed upstairs, you notice the room is shaking a bit.
Lights start to swing inside.

For MORE! Go to www.cambridge.org/elt/more and do a quiz on this text.

UNIT 9 If I had the money ...

In this unit

You learn
- second conditional
- *If I were you ...*
- indefinite pronouns *everyone, someone, no one, anyone*
- words for computers

and then you can
- give advice
- talk about people
- talk about what you would do

12 **1 Read and listen to the dialogue.**

Oliver I really need to buy a new laptop, but I haven't got enough money.

Claire Why do you need a new laptop?

Oliver Well, if I had a built-in DVD player, I could watch DVDs any time.

Karen If I were you, I'd use it to do more schoolwork.

Oliver Oh, come on! No one has said anything about my grades. If anyone had, I would have started working harder.

Rick What about Mr Sweeney?

Oliver What does he know? Everyone says he's too strict. I'd work harder if his lessons were more interesting. Anyway, if I had that notebook, I could work anywhere. Look, it's even got wireless LAN.

Karen Why don't you get a job?

Oliver Like what?

Karen Well, if you did a paper round, you'd earn some money.

Rick Hey, I've got an idea. There's always someone who needs help with a computer. Why don't you make some money that way?

Oliver Good idea, Rick! Would you like another orange juice?

2 **Match the sentence halves.**

1 Oliver really wants a new laptop
2 He wants to watch DVDs and to
3 Karen says he should
4 Oliver thinks he's working
5 If some classes weren't so boring,
6 Rick suggests he helps people
7 Oliver thinks this is

a do more schoolwork.
b by fixing their computers.
c he would work harder.
d but he hasn't got enough money.
e a brilliant idea.
f do a paper round.
g hard enough.

Get talking Giving advice

13 3 **Listen and repeat.**

Girl 1 I need to get more exercise.
Boy 1 If I were you, I'd go running every morning.
Girl 1 Hmm. But I hate running!

Boy 2 I need some extra money.
Girl 2 If I were you, I'd get a job at the café.
Boy 2 I can't, I'm too young.

4 **Match the expressions and the pictures.**

1 cut the grass
2 take a dog for a walk
3 wash cars
4 fix computers
5 do a paper round
6 do babysitting

5 **Work in pairs. Make dialogues like those from Exercise 3.**

A I need …

B If I were you, I'd …

Language Focus

Vocabulary Computer words

14 **1 Write the correct number of the words in the pictures. Listen and check.**

1 CD-ROM	3 mouse	5 notebook	7 modem	9 printer
2 flat screen	4 keyboard	6 DVD-R/W	8 USB stick	10 speakers

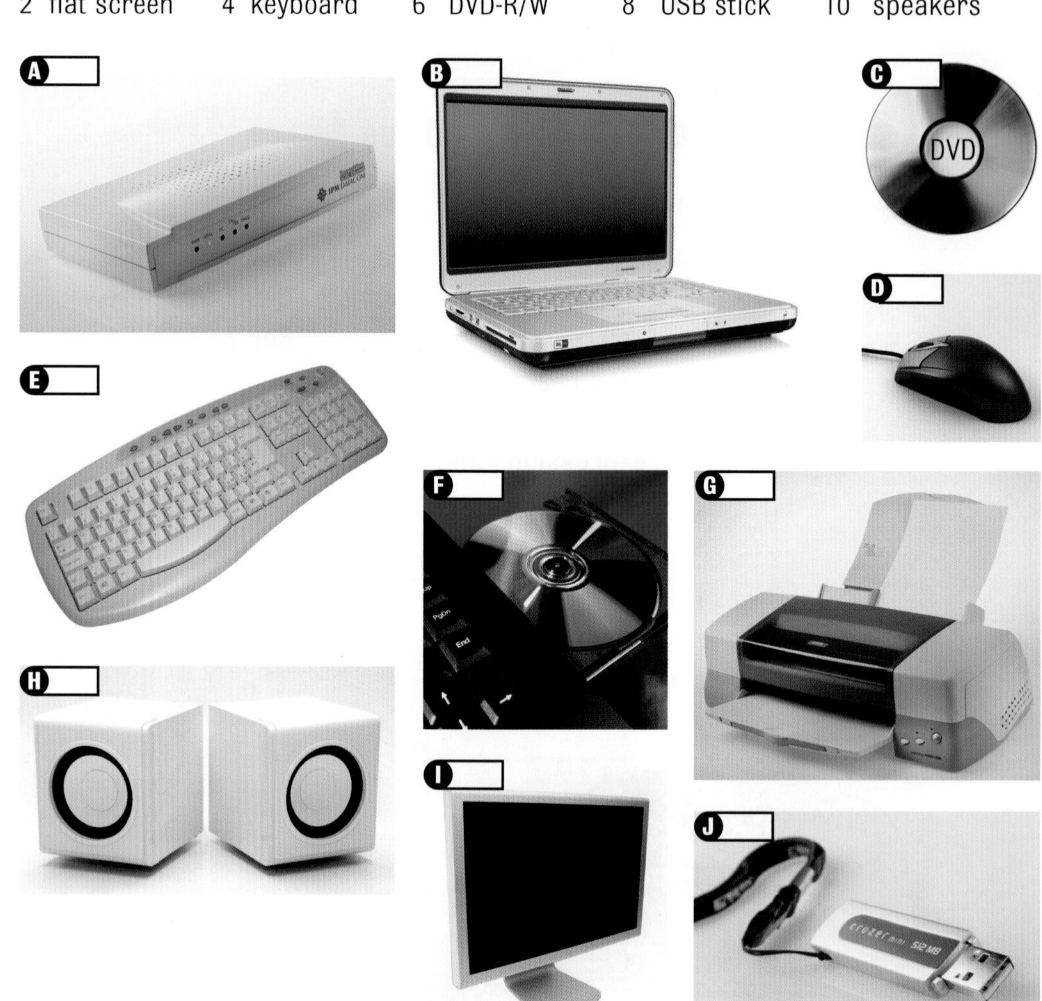

Get talking Talking about people

2 Work with a partner. A says one of the prompts, B has to finish it. Change roles.

1 I know someone who ....
2 At our school, everyone ....
3 In our class, there isn't anyone who ....
4 In our country, no one ....
5 I don't know anyone who ....
6 At our school, no one is allowed to ....
7 In our class, there is someone who ....
8 In Australia, everyone ....

Second conditional

1 **Put the verbs into the correct places then check with the dialogue on page 84.**

were could watch had 'd earn 'd work did

1 I .... harder if his lessons .... more interesting.
2 If you .... a paper round, you .... some money.
3 If I .... a built-in DVD player, I .... DVDs all the time.

The second conditional is used to talk about situations which are unreal.
Real: I don't have a notebook. I can't work anywhere.
Unreal: **If** I **had** a notebook, I **could** work anywhere.

Form:	**If clause**	**Main clause**
	If + past simple,	subject + would/wouldn't + base form of the verb.

2 **Circle the correct word.**

1 If I *have* / *had* more money, I'd buy it for you.
2 If you *go* / *went* to London, you'd learn a lot of English.
3 If it was my birthday today, *I'd get* / *I got* a lot of presents.
4 I would help you if I *didn't* / *wouldn't* have homework to do.
5 If he *would have* / *had* a girlfriend, he'd be very happy.
6 If there was a test tomorrow, I *wouldn't* / *didn't* pass it.

3 **Write the verbs in the correct form.**

1 I'd tell you the answer if I ....knew..... it myself! (know)
2 If I knew her phone number, I .... her. (phone)
3 If today .... Sunday, I'd still be in bed! (be)
4 If you were my friend, you .... me. (help)
5 You'd have more money if you .... a job. (get)

Get talking Talking about what you would do

4 **Work in pairs. Look at the prompts. Ask and answer.**

A What would you do if you lost your door key?

B I'd go to my friend's house. What would you do if ...?

lost your door key were headmaster of your school saw your teacher at the school disco
were angry with a friend saw a famous person felt ill

If I were you Giving advice

5 **Put the words into the correct order then check with the dialogue on page 84.**

If / you / I / I'd / to do schoolwork / were / use it

This is a special use of the Second Conditional: we use the phrase **If I were you** to introduce advice for another person.

A I've got toothache. **B If I were you,** I'd go and see a dentist.

6 **Match the sentences.**

1 My tooth hurts. ....
2 My grades are really bad. ....
3 I need some exercise. ....
4 I'm really tired. ....
5 My dog's sick. ....
6 The television doesn't work. ....

a If I were you, I'd go for a run.
b If I were you, I'd take it to the vet.
c If I were you, I'd phone the repair man.
d If I were you, I'd go to the dentist.
e If I were you, I'd study harder.
f If I were you, I'd go to bed early.

Indefinite pronouns *everyone, someone, no one, anyone*

7 **Complete the sentences then check with the dialogue on page 84.**

[1] .... has said anything about my grades.
[2] .... says he's too strict.
There's always [3] .... who needs help with a computer.
If [4] .... had, I'd have started working harder.

- Note that we can also say *everybody / somebody / nobody / anybody.*
- *no one / nobody* is only used with positive verb forms.
- *anyone / anybody* can be used with positive or negative verb forms:
  Anyone can do this. *I don't know anybody here.*

8 **Complete the sentences with the correct indefinite pronoun.**

1 We don't need a specialist for this job. ...Anyone... can do it!
2 When I got to Mike's house, ... was there, so I went home again.
3 I can't do this. I want .... to help me.
4 Everybody is invited. .... can come!
5 I don't know .... who likes her.
6 It was a great party. Mike was there, Jenny was there – .... was there!!

Get talking Asking about how long

I were you   Everyone in my class

15 **9** **Complete the dialogues with the phrases on the right. Listen and check.**

Craig I haven't finished my project yet.
Sonia Really? [1] .... has already finished.
Craig What can I do? If I had another two days, I'd do a great project.
Sonia If [2] .... I'd get something from the internet.
Craig Thanks. I'll do that.

Reading

1 Read the dilemmas and match them to the pictures.

Dilemma 1
Imagine your older brother asked you to give him an alibi for last night. He asked you to tell your parents he was with you.
What would you do?

Dilemma 2
Imagine someone broke the classroom window when your teacher wasn't there. When she returned she asked you who it was.
What would you do?

Dilemma 3
Imagine you were walking down the street and you found a wallet on the ground.
What would you do?

Listening

16 **2 Listen to Carla and Derek talking about the dilemmas in exercise 1. Circle T (true) or F (false).**

1 Carla's got two brothers. T / F
2 Carla would always give an alibi. T / F
3 Derek has got a good relationship with his brother. T / F
4 Carla would definitely tell the teacher. T / F
5 Derek wouldn't tell the teacher anything. T / F
6 Derek thinks it would be unfair if the teacher asked him. T / F
7 Carla would keep the wallet. T / F

Reading and speaking

 **Do the questionnaire. Tick your answers. Then discuss them.**

1 Imagine you were at a party. You took a picture off the wall to look at it. You dropped it and it broke. No one saw you do it. What would you do?

- ☐ I'd offer to fix it.
- ☐ I'd put it back on the wall and hope no one would notice.
- ☐ I'd leave it on the floor and go back to the party.

2 Imagine a friend of yours had some new glasses, and you thought they looked ridiculous. If your friend asked you for your opinion, what would you do?

- ☐ I would say I preferred my friend's old glasses.
- ☐ I would say they looked ridiculous.
- ☐ I would say they looked good.

3 Imagine you played in the school football team and the team was in the cup final. On the day of the game, you woke up and your leg was hurting. What would you do?

- ☐ I'd want to play, so I wouldn't say anything.
- ☐ I'd talk to the coach and ask for his advice.
- ☐ I wouldn't play.

4 Imagine you had the €150 you needed to buy a new bike. The same day your best friend phoned you and asked if he could borrow €150. What would you do?

- ☐ I'd lend him the money and buy a cheaper bike.
- ☐ I wouldn't give him the money.
- ☐ I'd tell him to talk to his parents about the problem.

5 Imagine you were having dinner at your friend's house and his mother gave you a plate with some vegetables that you really hate on it. What would you do?

- ☐ I'd tell her that I didn't like them.
- ☐ I'd leave them on the plate.
- ☐ I'd hide them in my coat pockets.

A Song 4 U If I were you

4 **Listen and complete the song with the words on the left.**

sad
would
were
goodbye (x2)
weren't
road
had
wheel

Oh my dear, if I [1]............. you
Then I wouldn't feel all blue,
Then I wouldn't feel all [2]............. ,
And I wouldn't feel so bad.

Chorus:
Turn the [3]............. back
Go and try
It won't work
I tell you [4].............
Turn the wheel back
Go and try
Everyone has got to say
Goodbye.

If I [5]............. another day,
I would surely like to stay.
If I had another year,
I [6]............. surely spend it here.

If my life [7]............. all mapped out,
If I had some little doubt
Where my [8]............. is leading to,
I would surely stay with you.

Oh my dear, if I were you,
Then I wouldn't feel all blue.
Life goes on, we wave [9]............. ,
Meet again maybe some day.

Writing for your Portfolio

5 **Write dilemma questions with three answers. Put all the dilemmas together and make a class questionnaire. Compare your answers.**

Example:
Imagine you borrowed a CD from a friend and you lost it.
What would you do?
I would buy another one.
I would hope he / she forgot about it.
I would say I was sorry.

Learn MORE through English

Number challenges

Key words

divide by	subtract	sum (or total)	row	horizontal
multiply by	a half	digit	column	
add (up)	circular	square	diagonal	

18

1 Work in pairs. Try to find the answers to these questions. Take notes. Then listen and check.

a What's 50 divided by a half?

b If there are three pizzas and you take away two, how many do you have?

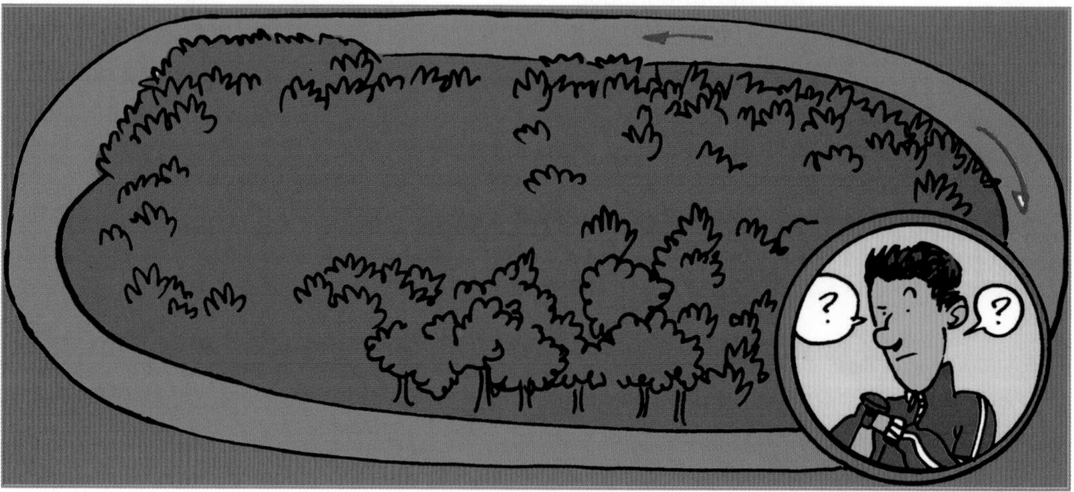

c A man lives next to a circular park. In the park, there are exactly 356 trees. Every morning, the man walks around the park. It takes him 80 minutes to walk around the park in a clockwise direction, but 1 hour 20 minutes to walk around it in an anti-clockwise direction. Why?

d You are driving a train from London to Glasgow. The train leaves at 11.00 and travels for 2 ¾ hours. There is a 20 minute stop in Birmingham, and a half hour stop in Manchester. Then the train continues for another 3 hours. What's the driver's name?

e Three friends have a meal at a restaurant together. The bill is £30, so each of them pays £10. Ten minutes later – the friends are still in the restaurant – the waiter notices a mistake with the bill. He charged £5 too much. So he takes £5 (in £1 coins) from the till to give to the three friends. On his way to their table, the waiter decides to keep £2 as a tip because it is difficult to divide £5 by 3. He gives each of the friends £1 back. So each of the friends paid £9. The waiter kept £2 – so the total is £29. What happened to the missing £1?

2 Practise this magic number trick yourself first. Then show it to a friend.

1 On a piece of paper, write the number NINE (in words). Do not show it to your friend. Fold the paper and put in an envelope. Seal the envelope and give it to your friend. Ask him/her not to open it yet.

2 Tell your friend to take a piece of paper and write down the last two digits of their phone number. Tell them to add the number of pounds (dollars, euros, pesos or whatever the currency in your country is) they have in their pocket to the last two numbers of their phone number.

3 Tell your friend to add his/her age, and the number of their house.

4 Tell them to subtract the number of brothers and sisters they have.

5 Tell them to subtract 12. Then add their favourite number.

6 Your friend should now multiply the total by 18.

7 Tell your friend to add up all the digits in the final total.

8 If the answer is more than 1 digit long, your friend should add up the digits again. (If necessary, your friend should do this until there is only one digit left).

9 Tell your friend that you know exactly what the answer is. Ask them to open the envelope and check.

19 **3** **Mini-project** Make a magic square for someone's birthday

1 If you are looking for a nice birthday present for someone you can create a magic square for them. The person must be older than 22. Lisa made this card for her mother, who is 37. Add up the numbers in every row and in every column. Then check the diagonal lines in the middle. Find out if Lisa got it right.

8	11	17	1
16	2	7	12
3	19	9	6
10	5	4	18

2 Can you create a magic square for someone? Remember the person has to be over 22. (But if you want to do it for a younger person, you can take another important number for them – e.g. the number of their house, if that is above 22).

3 To check and find out how you can do this, listen and take notes.

UNIT 10 Into the wilderness

1 Oliver is going to Botswana with his parents. Read the emails he writes to his friend Sam in Britain.

Hi Sam,

I'm going to spend my holidays in Botswana with my parents. "Where's that?" you'll ask. I'll tell you in a minute because I've checked it out. The story is that Mum and Dad are going to Botswana to show people how to use the water they have in a better way. Yesterday, they told me that I'm coming too. Brilliant! They have already had all their equipment flown out to Botswana. We're going next week, can you imagine? Cool! I'm so excited. You must be envious! (I didn't even protest when mum said yesterday, "Go and have your hair cut, Oliver! Nobody wants to go on holiday with hair like that!" #:-O)

See you,

Oliver

Botswana. Facts for dimwits like my friend Sam. (Just kidding!)

It's not in South Africa, it's in Africa - just north of South Africa in fact. It's almost two and a half times bigger than Great Britain. Any idea how many people live there? Well, I'll tell you: there are one and a half million! Imagine. There can't be a lot of towns and cities. Two and a half times the size of Britain, but only 1.5 million people. There are 60 million of us in Britain, in case you've forgotten. Most of Botswana is desert, so water must be a very important thing. The official language is – English! Most people speak English and Setswana. So, that's enough for your little head. Look at the map. Check out where Gabarone, the capital, is. That's where we're going to fly first.

In this unit

You learn

- to make deductions
- causative *have*
- words for holidays

and then you can

- give reasons
- talk about holiday plans
- make deductions

2 **Answer the questions below.**

1 Why are Oliver and his family going to Botswana?
2 What does Oliver have to do before he goes to Botswana?
3 How does Botswana compare to Britain (size and number of people)?
4 Why is water so important for people in Botswana?
5 What language(s) do people in Botswana speak?
6 What is the capital of Botswana?

Get talking Giving reasons

20 **3** **Listen and repeat.**

A Where do you want to go on holiday this year?
B I want to go to Africa.
A Why?
B To go on safari.

A Are you going on holiday this year?
B Yes, we want to go to Scotland.
A Why?
B To see the castles.

21 **4** **Match the pictures with the activities. Then listen and check.**

1 go on safari
2 go surfing
3 see Big Ben
4 go mountain climbing
5 have a camping holiday
6 go walking
7 go skiing
8 see the castles
9 go horseriding

A 
B 
C 
D 
E 
F 
G 
H 
I 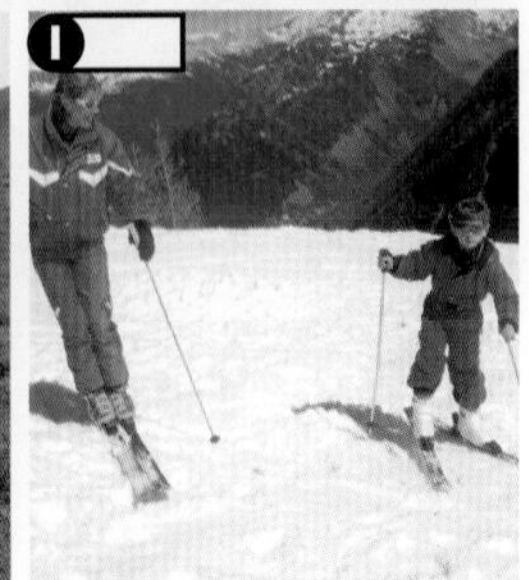

5 **Tick the activities you want to do on holiday and decide which of the places below is the best place to do them. Work with a partner and make up similar dialogues to those in Exercise 3.**

Africa Ireland Canada Australia Scotland England

Language Focus

Vocabulary Holiday words

book
buy
look at
make
find out
hire
check out
plan

22 **1 Listen and complete the phrases with the words on the left.**

1 .... a holiday
2 .... a trip
3 .... a hotel reservation
4 .... a car
5 .... a map of the area
6 .... the area .... on the web
7 .... what to do there
8 .... a dictionary

2 Work with a partner. A: Close your book. B: Ask four questions to see how many verbs A can remember. Change roles.

A What's number 3?
B make a hotel reservation

Get talking Talking about holiday plans

surfing
booked
holiday
made
camping

23 **3 Listen and complete the dialogue with the correct words.**

A Where are you going on [1] .... this year?
B We're going to Australia on a camping holiday.
I'm going to learn [2] .... and windsurfing.
A Cool! Have you [3] .... a flight yet?
B Yes, we have.
A Have you [4] .... a hotel reservation?
B No, we haven't. It's a [5] .... holiday!

Sounds right Question intonation

24 **4 Listen and repeat.**

A Have you got any plans for your holiday?
B Yes, I have.

A Have you booked your flight yet?
B No, I haven't.

5 Work with a partner. Talk about your holiday plans. Use the language below.

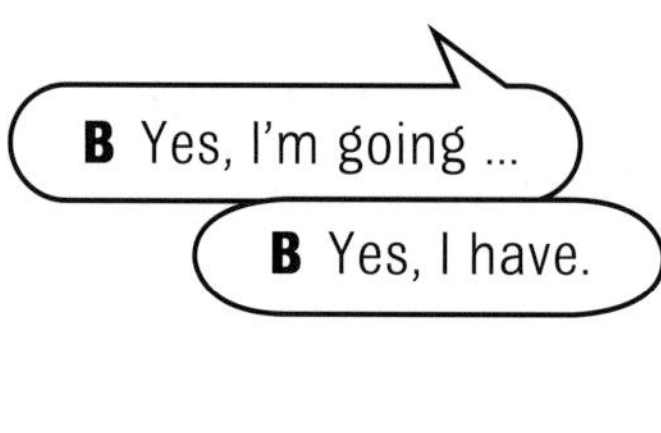

Grammar

Making deductions

1 **Complete the sentences with one word then check with the text on page 94.**

I'm so excited. You [1] .... be envious!
Only one and half million people – imagine. There [2] .... be a lot of towns and cities.

When you make a positive deduction, use *must*:
He won the match. He **must be** happy. (I'm sure that he <u>is</u> happy.)

When you make a positive deduction, use *can't*:
He lost the match. He **can't be** happy. (I'm sure that he <u>is not</u> happy.)

2 **Circle the correct option.**

1 She's got thirty birthday cards. She *must / can't* have a lot of friends.
2 He's calling from a public phone. His mobile phone *must / can't* be broken.
3 She doesn't speak Spanish. She *must / can't* be from Peru.
4 She looks very young. She *must / can't* be more than twenty.
5 He's got hundreds of CDs. He *must / can't* love music.
6 He didn't eat anything. He *must / can't* like pizza very much.

3 **Write deductions about these people. Use the words below to help you.**

1 happy
He must
be happy

2 old enough
....
....

3 very intelligent
....
....

4 hungry
....
....

5 Italian
....
....

Get talking Making deductions

4 **Work in pairs. A: choose sentences from column A. B: choose a suitable answer from column B. Change roles.**

A
I haven't eaten for six hours.
I have lost the CDs I bought yesterday.
Linda told me she's broken my MP3 player.
I'd like another burger.
Can you give me another sweater, please?

B
You've already eaten five. You can't be hungry.
You must be hungry.
You must be angry.
You must be sad.
You've already got three. You can't be cold.

Causative *have*

5 **Put the words in the correct order then check with the text on page 94.**

Go / your hair / and / cut / have
They / flown out / had / their equipment / have / to Botswana

We use this structure to say that another person does/did the action for us.
I had my hair **cut** last week. (= I did not cut it myself, another person cut it)
Form: Person + (form of the verb *have*) + object + past participle of the main verb.

6 **Complete the phrases with one of the verbs on the right.**

1 to have your hair ....
2 to have your room ....
3 to have your hair ....
4 to have your bike ....
5 to have a window ....
6 to have a carpet ....

cut
painted
fixed (2)
changed
dyed

7 **Look at the pictures and talk about what David and Hannah have done.**

A

He's had his hair cut ....

B

....
....

C

She's had her room painted ....

D

....
....

Infinitives of purpose

8 **Join the sentences together. Use *to* and *because*.**

1 Mary bought a new dress. She wants to wear it to the party.
Mary bought a new dress to wear to the party.
Mary bought a new dress because she wants to wear it to the party.
2 John phoned me. He wanted to invite me to the party.
3 Ben bought a new bike. He wanted to get some exercise.
4 I went to the newsagent's. I wanted to get the new *Cine Review* magazine.
5 Jill turned off the TV. She wanted to read a book.

Reading

1 Find out what happened to Oliver on his trip.

From: Oliver
To: Sam
Attachment:
Subject: News

Hi Sam,
Tuesday. Tomorrow we're going to fly from Gabarone to Maun. Mum's going to do some work with people in the desert for a few days and Dad's going to take me to the Okavango Delta for 6 days. The Okavango is a large wetland. I hope we see lions, leopards, buffalo, rhinos, elephants, giraffes, zebras, and crocodiles. I'm glad I brought my new camera with me. We're going to fly into the delta tomorrow on a small plane.
Cheers
Oliver

From: Oliver
To: Sam
Attachment:
Subject: News

Hi Sam,
Still Tuesday. You know what happened at lunch time? The window of my room in the hotel was open and I saw a man on the balcony next to our room. He had a black beard and was wearing sunglasses. He was making a phone call. I didn't hear everything, but one thing was clear: the man wanted to kill a leopard. :-o He said: "Okay. Let's meet in two days' time at Chitabe." That's a camp and it's where we're going!
CU
Oliver

From: Oliver
To: Sam
Attachment:
Subject: News

Hi Sam! Wednesday. The alarm clock rang at 5.30 this morning! "Get up, Oliver!" Dad said with a smile. "Today we're going to see the big five: a lion, a rhino, an elephant, a buffalo and a leopard!" he said. Dad looked like a five-year-old in front of the Christmas tree!
The flight was only half an hour and when I looked down everything looked great.
In the afternoon, we had our first trip in a Land Rover. First, we saw lots of elephants. When they slowly walked away, I saw some giraffes and zebras on the other side of the river. They were so cute, especially the young ones! I took lots of photos and then I suddenly saw my first leopard! What a great cat!

2 Read the text in Exercise 1 again. Then answer the questions.

1 What is the Okavango Delta?
2 What animals did Oliver hope to see in the delta?
3 What did Oliver hear in the hotel at lunch time?
4 What did the man look like?
5 How long did the flight into the delta take?
6 What animals did Oliver see on his first trip into the delta?

Listening

25 **3 Listen to Sam talking about Oliver's emails. Then complete the sentences.**

broken arm/ man had a cut on his head   the hotel / wanted to kill the leopard   arrested two men
the life of the leopard   ~~wanted to kill a leopard~~   wanted to come to their camp   a black car
the car before   control   landed on its roof

1 Oliver told Alex, the driver, about a man who *wanted to kill a leopard*..........
2 Oliver told Alex that the man ....
3 On the afternoon drive Alex suddenly saw ....
4 The other guide had never seen ....
5 The driver of the black car lost ....
6 The black car turned over and ....
7 One man had a .... and the other ....
8 The man with the broken arm was the man from .... who ....
9 The park rangers ....
10 Alex said that Oliver had saved ....

Writing for your Portfolio

4 Read the summary of part of Oliver's adventures in Botswana. Check with the text on page 99. Find and correct three mistakes.

On Thursday Oliver went to camp Chitabe in the Okavango Delta with his dad to see the animals. The day before they went Oliver heard three men talking about killing an elephant at the camp. He was worried. At the delta they saw lots of wonderful animals including a leopard.

5 Look at the script of the story. Write a summary of what happened next. Don't write more than 50 words.

Writing tips Summary writing

- Look at the text and underline the important information. This is the information that you really need to retell the story.
- Think about ways that you can make this information shorter. What words can you leave out?
- Rewrite the sentences. Don't use the sentences from the text.
- When you have finished, read your summary again to make sure that it is clear and easy to understand.

Check your progress Units 9 and 10

1 Reorder the letters and write words for parts of the computer.

1 semou ....
2 medom ....
3 nterpri ....
4 krsespea ....
5 boyekrda 5

2 Complete the phrases.

1 book a h _ _ _ _ _ _
2 plan a t _ _ _
3 make a r _ _ _ _ _ _ _ _ _ _
4 look at a m _ _
5 buy a d _ _ _ _ _ _ _ _ _ 5

3 Complete the dialogue with *everyone, someone, no one, anyone.*

A [1]............ knows Marco. He's very popular.
B When I arrived at this school last year. I didn't know [2]............... . Marco was the first person I spoke to.
A [3].............. likes their first day at school.
B It was terrible. I really needed [4]............... to talk to and I found Marco! 4

4 Complete using the second conditional.

1 I .... (go) if I ....(know) the address.
2 If they .... (have) more money, they .... (buy) the house.
3 If she ....(get) a job, she .... (be) happier.
4 We .... (help) them if they .... (need) it.
5 He ...... (learn) more English if he .... (go) to England.
6 If they .... (speak) more clearly, we .... (understand) them. 6

5 Complete the sentences with a verb and the causative *have*.

1 He .... his hair .... (cut) yesterday.
2 We .... our photos .... (take) there.
3 She .... her bag ....(steal)
4 They .... their car .... (check) today.
5 I always .... my papers .... (deliver)
6 She .... her scooter .... (fix) yesterday. 6

6 Write advice using *If I were you,...* and the verbs below.

1 .... (do a paper round)
2 .... (go out more)
3 .... (go running) 6

7 Write a deduction for each sentence.

1 I haven't had lunch. (hungry)
....
2 I've just passed my exams. (happy)
....
3 He's just lost his job. (pleased)
....
4 She's just opened the window. (hot)
....
5 You slept until 1 pm. (tired)
.... 10

8 Complete the sentences using *to* or *because*.

1 My dad lent me money .... I want to buy a car.
2 I went to the library .... I wanted a book.
3 He turned off the TV .... he needed to work.
4 My friend phoned .... invite me to the cinema. 8

TOTAL 50

My progress so far is ...

brilliant! ☐ quite good. ☐ not great. ☐

Gap Year Abroad

1 Read about *Raleigh International*, then answer the questions.

In 1978, Prince Charles started a two-year project called *Operation Drake*. Young people travelled around the world on a ship called the *Eye of the Wind*. The ship followed the route of the British explorer, Sir Francis Drake. The aim was to help young people develop self-confidence and leadership skills.

Operation Drake was very successful, so in 1984 Prince Charles started a bigger project called *Operation Raleigh*. It was named after the famous British explorer, Sir Walter Raleigh. This was a four-year project, and there were two ships and 4,000 volunteers who went around the world. The project was very popular so Prince Charles decided to make *Operation Raleigh* a permanent organization called *Raleigh International*.

Today young people (17 – 25 years old) from all backgrounds and all nationalities volunteer to work on *Raleigh International* projects. *Raleigh International* runs ten expeditions a year to Chile, Costa Rica, Nicaragua, Namibia and Malaysian Borneo.

1 Who were Prince Charles's projects named after?
2 Why did they decide to make *Operation Raleigh* a permanent organisation?
3 How old do you have to be to go on an expedition?
4 How many expeditions are there in a year?

Do YOU know?

After leaving school, many students in England choose to have a gap year before going to university. They take a year off to travel around Australia, Canada, America, Asia or Africa. Sometimes students join a programme like *Raleigh International*, *Greenforce* or *BUNAC*.

26

2 Listen and write the name of the correct organization under each photo.

Raleigh International   Gap Sports Abroad   Bunac

Organisation: ....

Organisation: ....

Organisation: ....

3 

What would you do if you had the opportunity? Interview your classmates and write who would do what.

Would you like to ..?
Yes, I would,/ No, I wouldn't. I would like to ...

MORE! And now you can watch *The School Magazine!* DVD

THE LEOPARD THAT LOST ITS SPOTS

If you count a leopard's spots
You'll find that it's got lots and lots.
(Only other leopards know
Just how many spots they grow.)

Lenny was a leopard small
Who one day heard his mother call:
'Lenny's ill! What has he got?
He's lost his biggest, blackest spot!'
Poor Lenny hunted high and low,
Just where it was he didn't know.
The other leopards looked around,
But still the spot could not be found.

Now in the jungle lived a man,
And down to him young Lenny ran.
He told him of his missing spot.
The man said, 'I know what I've got!'
He went into his grassy den
And came out with a little pen.

Soon Lenny ran back home again,
His visit had not been in vain.
Upon his back, what do you think?
A brand new spot in thick, black ink!
The leopards thanked the man who plotted
To make their Lenny fully spotted!

For MORE! Go to www.cambridge.org/elt/more and do a quiz on this text.

UNIT 11 He told us not to worry

In this unit

You learn

- reported speech
- *want/ask/tell* someone to do something
- words for the environment

and then you can

- say what you want people to do

27 **1 Read and listen to the dialogue.**

Karen Did you hear about the park?

Claire No. What about it?

Karen They say that they want to cut down some of the trees and make it much smaller. They want to build a car park and they need part of the park for the entrance – the part near South Street.

Claire But that means we can't play there any more.

Karen I know! I want you to go and talk to other kids in the park then we can decide on a plan of action.

(*The next day*)

Karen Oliver and I went to the city council yesterday and talked to a city planner. He told us they are going to do it. He told us not to worry. He said that we'll still have half the park to play in!

Claire That's true but there's no playing field in the other half.

Karen I know! Work's going to start in a month. He asked us to support the city council. But I want to organise a protest march through the park.

Rick What about a petition? We can ask people to sign it!

Karen Good idea!

2 **Match the sentence halves.**

1 Karen says that they want to cut down
2 She says that they want to build
3 Karen says that she
4 Oliver and Karen go to the city council
5 The city planner wants them to
6 They want to write a petition,

a wants the others to talk to other people in the park.
b and speak to a city planner there.
c trees and make the park smaller.
d support the city council.
e and organise a protest march.
f a car park.

Get talking Saying what you want people to do

28 **3** **Listen and repeat.**

A I want you to do something for me.
B What is it?
A I want you to post a letter.
B OK, I'll do that straightaway.

A I want you to do something for me.
B What is it?
A I want you to come to the shops.
B I'm sorry, I can't. I have to do my homework.

29 **4** **Match the phrases with the pictures. Listen and check.**

1 do the washing up
2 buy me an ice cream
3 do my maths homework
4 post a letter
5 do the shopping
6 lend me some money

A 
B 
C 
D 
E 
F 

5 **Work with a partner. Make dialogues like the ones from Exercise 3. Use the ideas from the pictures above.**

Language Focus

Vocabulary The environment

1 Match the phrases and the pictures

2 Read the questionnaire and circle your answers. See how "green" you are.

What's your green score?

1 I (a) always (b) sometimes (c) hardly ever (d) never save water.
2 I (a) always (b) sometimes (c) hardly ever (d) never take glass bottles to the bottle bank.
3 I (a) never (b) hardly ever (c) sometimes (d) always throw paper and plastic bottles in the street.
4 When leaving the beach I (a) never (b) hardly ever (c) sometimes (d) always leave litter behind.
5 I (a) always (b) sometimes (c) hardly ever (d) never put paper into special containers to be recycled.
6 I (a) always (b) sometimes (c) hardly ever (d) never ask my parents to drive me short distances.

Results

You ticked (a) at least four times: You are really "green".
You ticked (b) at least four times: You are quite "green". Keep up the effort.
You ticked (c) at least four times: You probably know what you should do, but you are too lazy.
You ticked (d) at least four times: You are a litter bug. You are not "green" at all.

Grammar

Reported speech

1 **Look at the dialogue on page 104 and complete the examples.**

He [1] .... are going to do it.
He [2] ....'ll still have half of the park to play in.

2 **Complete the rule with *say* or *tell***

When we report what people say, we often use the verbs *say* and *tell*.
[1] .... is not followed by an object.
[2] .... is followed by an object.

Make sure you change the pronoun.
Helen said, "**You** look sad." – She said that **I** look sad.
Bob said, "**We** might be late" – He said **they** might be late.
Trevor said, "It's **my** birthday." – He told us that it's **his** birthday.

3 **Circle the correct option.**

1 He *says / says me* that he doesn't speak English very well.
2 They *told / told us* they were Spanish.
3 She *told / told her* she wasn't coming.
4 He *says / says him* he wants more French fries.

4 **Complete the sentences.**

1 "I'm hungry," says Paul.
Paul says that *he is hungry*.
2 "We're going home," Jenny tells me.
Jenny tells me ...
3 "I'm not happy," says Sue.
Sue ...
4 "You look like my sister," the girl tells me.
The girl ...
5 "You are tired!" she tells us.
She ...
6 "They are going to sell the house," May says. May ...

want/ask/tell someone to do something

We often use the verb *want* with an object pronoun + *to*.

I want **you** to go and talk to other kids in the park.
I **don't** want **you** to tell anyone.

The verbs *ask* and *tell* have a similar construction in the negative form. Note the position of *not*.
He told us **not to** worry.
He **asked** me **not to** tell anyone.

5 **Match the sentences and the pictures.**

1 He wants you to take him for a walk.
2 I want you to go to sleep now.
3 He asked me to marry him.
4 She asked me not to drive so fast.
5 She told him not to run.
6 He told me to be quiet.

6 **Put the words in order to make sentences.**

1 help / He / to / him / asked / me — *He asked me to help him.*
2 buy / She / to / some / him / milk / asked ....
3 say / They / not / me / to / anything / asked ....
4 I / for / her / to / told / me / wait ....
5 not / We / them / to / anything / touch / told ....
6 with / He / wanted / to / me / him / go ....

7 **Make the sentences negative.**

1 I want you to turn off the TV. — *I don't want you to turn off the TV.*
2 He told me to leave. ....
3 We asked them to be there at 5 pm. ....
4 She told us to buy some bread. ....
5 Dave wants us to arrive early. ....
6 I told them to play in the garden. ....

30 **8** **Complete the dialogues with the sentences. Listen and check. Then act it out.**

Sandra Gerry?
Gerry What is it, Sandra?
Sandra I want you [1]..........
Gerry What is it?
Sandra [2].......... me they are planning to build a motorway through our village.
Gerry Through the village? That's ridiculous!
Sandra Exactly. [3].......... work's going to start next month. That's why [4].......... to help me.
Gerry Help you with what?
Sandra We want to [5].......... a petition, and [6].......... leaflets to all the people in the village.
Gerry That's a brilliant idea.
Sandra Will you help us?
Gerry Of course.

Someone told
write
give
I want you
He said
to do something for me

9 **Choose one of the situations below and write a short dialogue like the one in Exercise 6. Then act it out.**

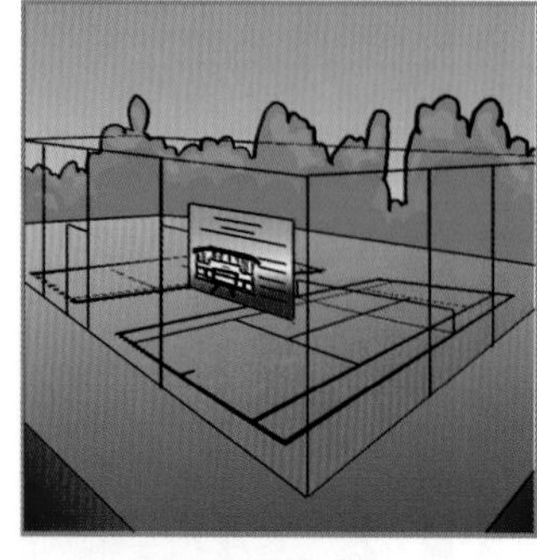

There are plans to build a supermarket where the tennis courts are.

Children are not allowed to use school computers for their project work.

The school library is not open in the afternoon any more.

They want to fill in the pond in the park.

Skills

Reading and writing

1 **Read about these people who stood up for their rights and answer the questions below.**

ECONOMY vs ECOLOGY

Those who speak up may find it difficult.

Wangari Maathai. Wangari Maathai (b. 1940) from Kenya won the Nobel Peace Prize in 2004 for her fight for democracy and for the environment. She was the first African woman to win the prize.

Maathai founded the Green Belt Movement in Kenya in 1977, which has planted more than 10 million trees. She has been to prison many times because of her fight for the rights of women and because of her work for the environment. In 2002, she won a seat in the Kenyan parliament.

Erin Brockovich. In the early 1990's, Erin Brockovich (b. 1960), a single mother of three, was working for a law firm. While organising papers one day, she discovered that many people who lived in and around Hinkley California in the 1960's, 70's and 80's were seriously ill. She later found out that there was poison in the water. It came from a gas and electricity company. In 1996, she and lawyer Ed Masry won $333 million for more than 600 people from Hinkley.

Swampy. In 1995, the British government started building roads through different areas of England. One of the most controversial was the road near Newbury, a town about 60 miles from London. Eco-warriors objected to the road as it destroyed an area of ancient woodland. These protesters lived in tree houses along the route and built camps and dug tunnels in the ground. The most famous of these eco-warriors was Swampy. He refused to come out of his tunnel in the ground for 167 hours when police came to move the protesters away. However, the road was built although the government stopped its road building programme soon after.

1 What does the Green Belt Movement in Kenya do?
2 Who won the Nobel Peace Prize in 2004?
3 What did Erin Brockovich discover about Hinkley, California?
4 What is an eco-warrior?
5 Were the eco-warriors successful in stopping road building in England?

2 **Summarise what each of these people did in one sentence.**

Listening

31 **3 Listen to these students talking about their favourite heroes/heroines. Complete the table.**

	Hannah	John	Natasha
Who?	*Mahatma Gandhi*		
Why?			

Speaking

4 In pairs talk about your heroes. Then tell the class.

One of my heroes is ....
I admire him/her because ....
I think it is/was really great, the way she/he ....
I think it's great that she/he ....
She/He usually ....
Once she/he ....
I admire how much .... she/he has.

Writing for your Portfolio

5 Design a leaflet for something you want to stand up for.

Make sure you:

- find a good slogan
- say what it is all about
- say what you are planning to do

MAKE CYCLING SAFE!
Say **yes** to a
new cycling path!!
Ride to the next meeting and join our
PROTEST RIDE
to the Town Hall!
Saturday, 3 pm
in front of the old school
Keep on riding!

A Song 4 U We shall overcome

32 **6 Can you name either of the people in the photos? Listen to the song.**

We shall overcome,
We shall overcome,
We shall overcome some day.

Chorus:
Oh deep in my heart,
I do believe,
We shall overcome some day.

We'll walk hand in hand,
We'll walk hand in hand,
We'll walk hand in hand some day.

Chorus

We shall all be free,
We shall all be free,
We shall all be free some day.

Chorus

We are not afraid,
We are not afraid,
We are not afraid today.

Chorus

We are not alone,
We are not alone,
We are not alone today.

Chorus

The whole wide world around,
The whole wide world around,
The whole wide world around some day.

Chorus

We shall overcome,
We shall overcome,
We shall overcome some day.

Chorus

Energy and how to save it

Key words

energy consumption
(energy-saving) light bulb
average temperature
(powering and lighting) appliances

stove
heat
blackout
increase

petrol pump
solar panel
wind turbine
tide

renewable energy
(marine) current
source (of energy)
insulation

1 Energy consumption. Read the text.

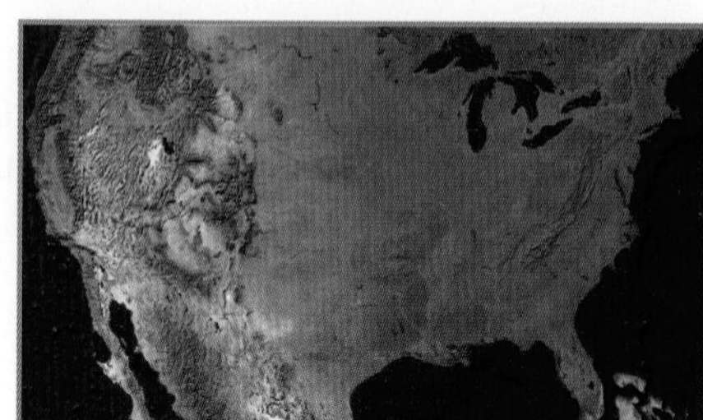

If you look at North America from space at night you can see how developed countries light up the world.

Imagine the following situation. It's nine o'clock at night in New York. Suddenly there is a blackout in the eastern states of the USA. Underground trains stop. TV screens go blank, washing machines stop, everything is dark. Blackouts happen because more and more people use more and more energy. In the last 40 years, energy consumption has increased by 250%. Scientists think that by the year 2030 energy use will have doubled. And that will cause great problems.

33 **2 How do we use energy at home?**
Guess what people in Great Britain used energy for in 2002. Then listen and check.

1 cooking	About 61%
2 lighting and powering appliances	About 23%
3 heating water	About 13%
4 heating rooms in the house	About 3%

3 Space heating.

The picture on the right shows how energy is lost. In the picture, energy is lost through the windows and walls.

Look at the average temperatures in British homes since 1970. What was the increase? 20%, 35% or 50%?

1970	12.6C
1990	16.9C
2001	18.9C

4 Energy alternatives and saving energy. Read the text.

Solar panels are already being used to power petrol pumps at a petrol station in Perivale, United Kingdom. Especially in hot countries, solar power will be one of the most important sources of renewable energy. Experts in Namibia have developed a stove which uses the sun as a source of energy.

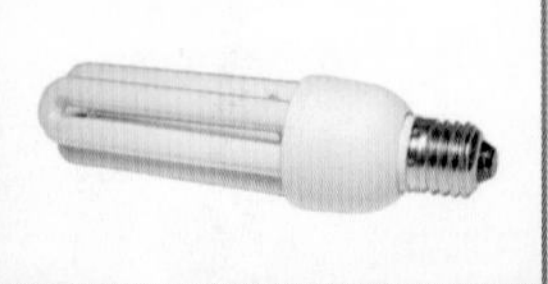

Energy-saving light bulbs use only a fifth of what traditional bulbs use.

Insulation helps to reduce the energy consumption of old houses. When a new house is built, the temperature in the house is higher if the house faces south, and if there is a lot of glass that catches the sun.

There are about 2000 wind turbines in Great Britain. They produce renewable energy, but there is a problem. There have been protests because some people think that they make beautiful landscapes look ugly.

There are currents in the sea because of the tides. When we use underwater turbines (in much the same way that a wind turbine works), we can make electricity. The advantage is that this form of energy is always there. Work is going on to develop marine current turbines. These could be built in groups under the sea, like an underwater wind farm.

Think about how you get to school. More and more children are driven to school by their parents. You can save energy if you walk or cycle to school.

Mini-project Saving energy

5 Check the internet or the library for facts about how you can save energy. Design a leaflet, including facts, advice and illustrations about how to save energy in your home or school.

UNIT 12 California

1 **Read about California.**

California

Here we come!

"We are in the Joshua Tree National Park in the desert. It's amazing – the shapes of the trees are just incredible. Some look like strange animals!"

" We are in Universal Studios today! It's brilliant! There's an earthquake and you get attacked by the shark from *Jaws*!! We also want to go to the Walk of Fame where lots of famous actresses and actors have a pink star in the pavement!"

California STATE OF CONTRASTS!

by Steven Doyle

Last month, I decided to visit and experience California, one of the USA's most popular and famous states. At my hotel, I met David and Emma from London. I asked them why they were here. They said they were on holiday there with their parents and they told me they were going to the Joshua Tree National Park that day. I saw them later in the evening. They said that the park was amazing. I wanted to know if they planned to visit again. They said they wanted to as there were still so many things to see like Yosemite National Park and San Francisco.

That's the thing about California. It's so diverse with mountains, deserts and famous places like Venice Beach. Of course, its main attraction must be Hollywood. Thousands of people go there every year to visit the Walk of Fame in Los Angeles and to experience their favourite films at Universal Studios. I met Jane and Sarah at the hotel who told me their visit to Universal Studios was one of the best days of their life! So if you want to go to a great place with lots of different things to see and do, visit The Sunshine State of California!

In this unit

You learn
- reported speech 2
- words for physical appearance

and then you can
- justify options
- identify a person

2 Circle T (True) or F (False) for the sentences below.

1 California is known as the Golden State. T / F
2 There are no deserts in California. T / F
3 There is a national park in California. T / F
4 California has lots of different scenery. T / F
5 There is a film studio in California. T / F
6 San Francisco and New York are in California. T / F

Get talking Justifying opinions

34 **3 Listen to the sentences and practise saying them.**

1 I love American people. They are so friendly.
2 Universal Studios is wonderful. It's fun and interesting.

35 **4 Match the sentences. Listen and check, then practise saying them.**

1 The beaches in America are fantastic.
2 The mountains in Yosemite National Park are amazing.
3 San Francisco is great.
4 California is a very friendly place.
5 Santa Cruz is a cool city on the coast.

a It's an amazing city and there's always something to do there.
b There's always a big welcome there for you.
c They're really clean and the sand is beautiful.
d It's got some great beaches.
e They're so high.

5 Make a list of countries and cities you know well. Tell your partner about them and justify your opinions.

London is a bit boring. It's always raining there.

New York is an exciting city. There's lots of things to do there.

Language Focus

Vocabulary Physical appearance

hair
body
~~eyes~~
clothes
hair

36 **1 Complete the lists with the words on the left. Listen and check.**

1 grey / blue / brown / green ......*eyes*..........
2 curly / straight / short / long / thin / ....
3 tall / short / plump / thin / slim / well-built / muscular ....
4 casual / elegant / smart / scruffy / torn / dirty / sporty ....
5 blonde / red / grey/ brown / white / black / dyed ....

Get talking Identifying a person

2 Work in pairs. Choose a person in the picture. Describe what he or she looks like. Your partner points to the correct person in the picture.

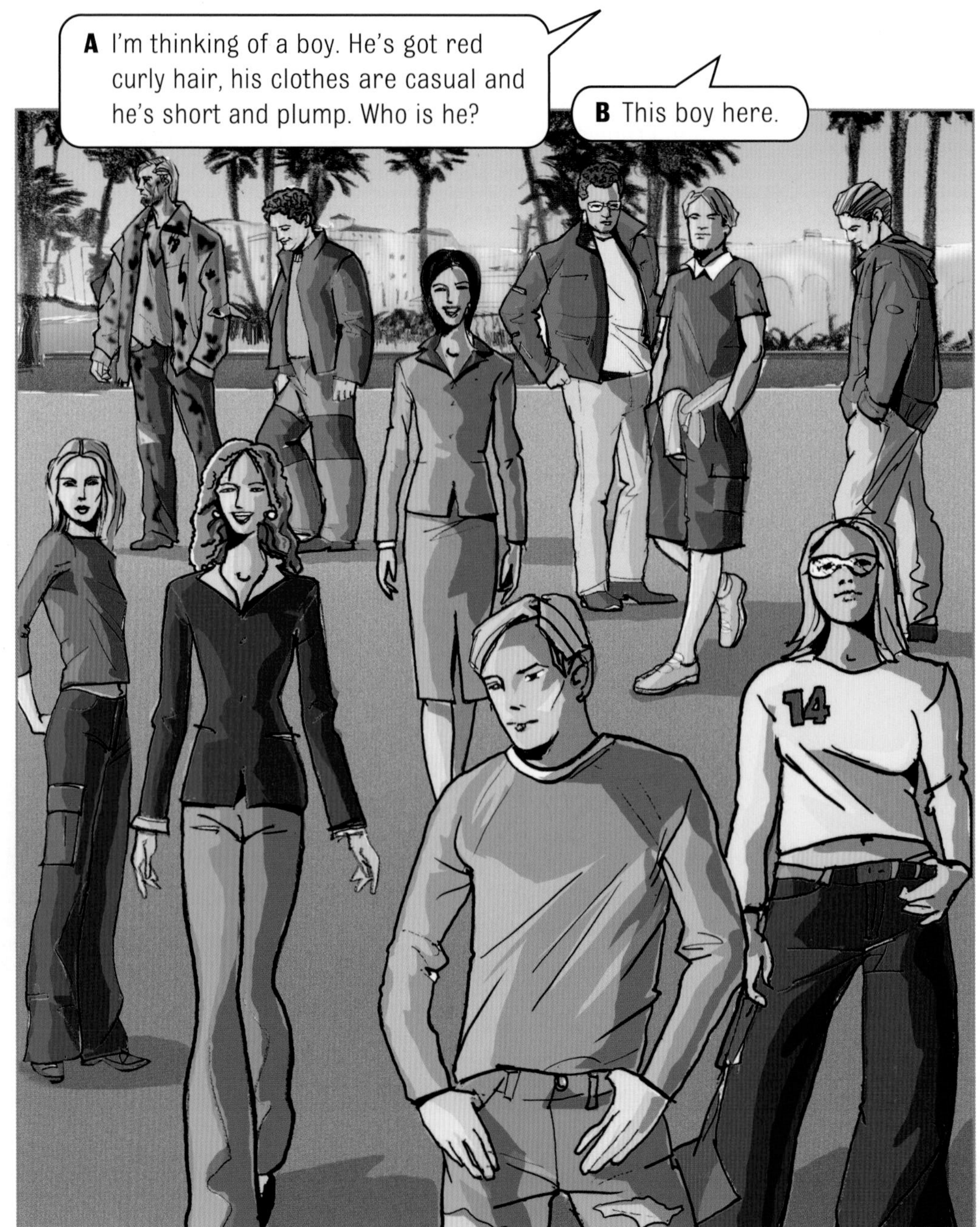

Grammar

Reported speech 2

1 **Complete the sentences then check with the text on page 114.**

1 'We want to visit again.' → They .... they .... to visit again.
2 'Why are you here?' → I asked them .... they .... here.
3 'Do you plan to visit again?' → I wanted to know .... they .... to visit again.

- When we report someone's words, we often change the verb tense: see sentences 1, 2 and 3.
- When we report a question, we use the same question word (*who/what/why* etc.): see sentence 2.
- When we report a *Yes/No* question, we use the word *if*: see sentence 3
- When we report questions, we don't use *do/does/did* or the question word order: see sentences 2 and 3

2 **Circle the correct form of the verbs.**

1 Joanne says that she *likes / liked* travelling.
2 Barbara told me that she *is going / was going* to Australia for a holiday.
3 Our friends said that they *are staying / were staying* in a nice hotel.
4 He said he *doesn't like / didn't like* the beaches in Santa Monica.
5 I said I *am / was* very happy.
6 They tell us that they *love / loved* the sun.
7 She says that she *has / had* no time.
8 You told me you *write / wrote* ten emails a day.

3 **Present or past? Complete the sentences with the correct form of the verbs.**

1 She told me that her uncle .... on a farm. (live)
2 She says she .... ice cream. (not like)
3 They told us that the weather .... great. (be)
4 Tony says he .... very happy about this. (be)
5 He says he never .... DVDs at home. (watch)
6 They told us that they .... in San Diego. (be)
7 Caroline said that she .... Carl. (love)

4 **Complete the sentences. Choose the correct question word.**

where ~~why~~ how much if (x3)

1 She said, "Why are you angry?"
She wanted to know ....*why*..... I was angry.
2 He said, "Do you watch a lot of TV?"
He asked her .... she watched a lot of TV.
3 They asked me, "Are you a student?"
They wanted to know .... I was a student.
4 She asked, "Where's your brother?"
She asked .... my brother was.
5 He said, "Do you like sport?"
He asked .... I liked sport.
6 She asked, "How much are the pink jeans?"
She asked me .... the pink jeans were.

Game

5 **Work in groups of four. Each member of the group needs four strips of paper. Write a different sentence about yourself on each strip of paper. Add your first name. Two must be true and two must be lies. All four sentences must be in the Present tense. Hand out your strips of paper to the other members of the group.**

Meg said that she was going to Turkey for a holiday. I think that's a lie.

No, it's not a lie, it's true.

Sounds right Word stress

37 **6** **Listen to the stress in these words then write them in the correct column. Listen again and check.**

A □▢□□	**B** □□▢□
....	....
....	....
....	....
....	....

politician
information
education
incredible
photographer
European
American
identify

38 **7** **Listen and repeat.**

1 He's an American photographer.
2 I had an incredible education.
3 She's a European politician.
4 I can't identify the information.

Skills

Reading

1 Read the texts. Put the phrases A-D in the correct places.

A This is a place where
B the stars aren't only humans
C don't forget to go on
D a bit more contemporary

+ - / http://www.latb

Los Angeles – some 'must do' sightseeing things for visitors.

1 Hollywood. Walk along the Walk of Fame – see the stars and the hand-prints in the pavement of many famous people, like Marilyn Monroe and Elvis Presley. They're on Hollywood Boulevard and Vine Street. (And ☐ ! You can even see the 'paw-prints' of Lassie, the film-star dog of the 1950s!)

2 Visit Universal Studios! This is one of the most famous film studios in Hollywood. See where and how some of the great movies of all time were made, meet King Kong and Terminator 2 – and ☐ the Jurassic Ride (which includes a 25m drop at one point!)

3 Go to Venice Beach. Walk along the sidewalks in Venice Beach, watch the skateboarders or just sit and eat an ice cream. Hire a bicycle and go cycling. ☐ you might see some famous movie stars!

4 Spend the day at The California Adventure. This is Disney's latest park, beside Disneyland in Anaheim, but it's ☐ than Disneyland itself. There are some great rides (like 'California Screaming') but also lots of cool information about the state of California (its history, its parks, its people).

Speaking

2 Imagine you have just come back from Los Angeles. Interview each other about what you did.

1 Where did you go?
2 How long did you stay?
3 Did you have a good time?
4 Did you meet any interesting people?

A Song 4 U California dreaming

3 **Listen and complete the song with the words on the left.**

church	tell
sky	knees
leave	walk
cold	warm
leaves	day

All the leaves are brown.
and the [1]........................ is grey.
I've been for a [2]........................
on a winter's day.
I'd be safe and [3]........................
if I was in L.A.
California dreaming,
on such a winter's [4].........

I stopped into a [5]........................
I passed along the way.
Well, I got down on my [6]................
and I began to pray.
You know, the preacher likes the
[7]........................ ,
he knows I'm gonna stay.
California dreaming,
on such a winter's day.

All the [8]........................are brown,
and the sky is grey.
I've been for a walk
on a winter's day.
If I didn't [9]........................ her,
I could [10]........................ today.
California dreaming,
on such a winter's day.

Writing for your Portfolio

4 **Imagine you are in California. Write a letter to your English penfriend describing what you are doing and the places you have visited. You will find plenty of ideas by looking back through the unit and by finding out some more things about California on the Internet.**

I am sitting on the beach writing this letter. I can see ...
Yesterday we went to Hollywood, it was ...
On Monday ...
San Francisco is really exciting ...
The best place was ...

Check your progress Units 11 and 12

1 Complete the sentences.

1 Don't be a l _ _ _ _ _ lout.
2 R _ _ _ _ _ _ paper.
3 R _ _ _ your bike.
4 S _ _ _ water.
5 Bring your own b _ _ _ _ _ .

5

2 Complete the sentences.

1 His hair isn't curly. It's s _ _ _ _ _ _ _ _ .
2 Her clothes are terrible and sc _ _ _ _ _ _ .
3 He always wears sm _ _ _ suits.
4 She has got dy _ _ hair.
5 He exercises a lot and is very mu _ _ _ _ _ _ _.
6 She isn't fat or thin. She is p _ _ _ _ .
7 She always looks nice and e _ _ _ _ _ _ _ .

7

3 Write sentences using *want someone to do something.*

1 A: ....
B: OK. I'll do the washing-up.
2 A: ....
B: OK. Tom will help you with your maths homework.
3 A: ....
B: OK. Sue will do the shopping.

6

4 Complete the sentences with the correct pronoun.

1 Mark: 'I'm angry.' Mark says .... is angry.
2 Rachel: ' We're going on holiday tomorrow.' Rachel says .... are going on holiday tomorrow.
3 Sue: 'You (pl) are hungry!' Sue says .... are hungry.
4 Tom: 'They are going to buy a new scooter.' Tom says .... are going to buy a new scooter.

4

5 Circle the correct form of the verb.

1 He *told / said* that he didn't like her.
2 They *told / tells* me they were leaving.
3 She *says / tells* that she is happy.
4 He *tells / says* us he is tired.

4

6 Write the sentences in the negative form.

1 I want you to come tomorrow.
....
2 They told me to go.
....
3 We asked them to play on the grass.
....
4 She told us to go home.
....
5 He wants them to leave.
....

10

7 Complete the sentences using indirect speech.

1 She told me her mother .... (be) a teacher.
2 He says he .... (live) near me.
3 They said that they .... (like) ice cream.
4 He tells them he .... (want) some money.

4

8 Rewrite the sentences using indirect speech.

1 'Do you like pizza?' he asked me.
....
2 'Where do you go to school?' she asked him.
....
3 'How much money is there?' he asked me.
....
4 'Are you a teacher?' they asked her.
....
5 'Why are you angry?' he asked them.
....

10

TOTAL 50

My progress so far is ...

brilliant! ☐ quite good. ☐ not great. ☐

Learn MORE about Culture

What a waste!

1 Listen and then answer the questions about plastic.

1 What is the problem with plastic?
2 How long will plastic stay in the rubbish tip?
3 Why don't companies want to buy plastic for recycling?
4 What is *Mater-Bi* made of?
5 What is different about *Mater-Bi*?

Do YOU know?

A lot of the waste produced in the western world is plastic. Most of the food and drink we buy in supermarkets is packed in plastic — in some countries plastic is twenty per cent of all waste. All of the electronic and electrical appliances we use (such as fridges, mobile phones and laptops) use plastic. Plastic is very difficult to get rid of.

2 Read the text and complete the chart.

Each year in Europe, about 100 million new mobile phones are bought. There are about 85 million old phones lying in cupboards in people's homes. What a waste!

In 2003, the *Eazyfone Group* started the *Fones4schools* campaign in the UK. Now, about 800,000 school children hand in their old mobile phones. In return, the school receives some money. The phones are then recycled.

Easyfone separates the phones into three groups: phones for reuse, phones for repair and phones for recycling.

Phones for Recycling
There are some valuable materials in mobile phones such as gold, silver and copper. The metals are taken out and reused in jewellery, copper pipes or new mobile phones. The plastic is reused in traffic cones or printer cassettes.

Phones for Reuse and Repair
Handsets are very expensive and in some countries in Africa and Eastern Europe, people cannot afford them. Phones are sent to these countries and they are given or resold cheaply.

Check out mobile phone recycling on the *envocare* website and see if there is a scheme near you.

How many mobile phones do Europeans buy every year?
1...

How many old phones are lying in cupboards in people's houses?
2...

How many children take part in the *Fones4schools* campaign?
3...

How are the phones recycled?
4...

What happens to the phones for reuse?
5...
....

3 Over 2 U! In pairs, plan a recycling scheme for your class or school.

MORE! And now you can watch *The School Magazine!*

The sound of California

One of the hottest states in the USA has been providing some of the hottest pop and rock music for over half a century. Here are some of the most famous artists from the sunshine state.

The 1960s

Forget the Beatles and the Rolling Stones! Many critics will tell you that the most influential band in rock history is, in fact, The Beach Boys. The band was started in 1961 in Hawthorne, California, by brothers Brian, Carl and Denis Wilson, with their cousin Mike Love and friend Alan Jardine.

Their early songs were all about being young in California, things like the sun, beaches, and cars (*Fun, Fun, Fun, Little Deuce Coupe*) and surfing (*Surfin' Safari, Surfin' USA*). But as the band got older their songs became more sophisticated.

During the mid 1960s the band produced their greatest album *Pet Sounds* and the single *Good Vibrations*, which is considered by many people as the greatest single of all time.

The 1970s

The Eagles were formed in the early 1970s in Los Angeles. Over the next ten years they became the best-selling American band of all time with five number one singles and four number one albums. Their *Greatest Hits* album has sold more copies worldwide than any other album except Michael Jackson's *Thriller*.

They are famous for their easy-listening country style rock made popular in songs like *Take It Easy, Lying Eyes, Life in the Fast Lane* and, of course, *Hotel California*.

The band broke up in 1980 but got back together again in 1994 for a series of hugely successful shows around the world. They have also started to record new music to introduce a new generation of fans to the sound of Southern California.

The new millennium

In 2006 Red Hot Chili Peppers showed that they really are the biggest Californian band on the planet when their new CD, *Stadium Arcadium*, went straight into the charts at number one in 27 countries around the world. The band started in 1983 when former Fairfax High School students, Michael 'Flea' Balzary (bass), Anthony Kiedis (vocals), Jack Irons (drums) and Hillel Slovak (guitar) got together.

They first played under the name Tony Flow and the Miraculously Majestic Masters of Mayhem. Less than a year later they were really popular on the Los Angeles rock scene and signed a deal with EMI. Since then, they have released nine studio albums and played to millions of fans all over the world.

With their mixture of alternative rock, punk, rap, funk and heavy metal, Red Hot Chili Peppers have created what many people consider to be the sound of modern California.

And the future? These days there are plenty of new up-and-coming bands coming from California. Bands like Black Rebel Motorcycle Club, The Warlocks and Scarling. You haven't heard of them yet but wait a few years. And even if none of these make it big, you can be sure that it won't be long before the next big band from California hits the music world.

For MORE! Go to www.cambridge.org/elt/more and do a quiz on this text.

Wordlist

Unit 1

ages /ˈeɪdʒɪz/
argument /ˈɑːgjumənt/
to breathe /tə ˈbriːð/
to brighten up /tə ˌbraɪtn ˈʌp/
by the way /ˌbaɪ ðə ˈweɪ/
cell /sel/
cough /kɒf/
deadly /ˈdedli/
to desert /tə dɪˈzɜːt/
digital camera /ˌdɪdʒɪtl ˈkæmərə/
drop /drɒp/
ever /ˈevə(r)/
fall /fɔːl/
to fancy doing /tə ˌfænsi ˈduːɪŋ/
fever /ˈfiːvə(r)/
flat /flæt/
flu /fluː/
games console /ˈgeɪmz ˌkɒnsəʊl/
to get in touch with /tə ˌget ˌɪn ˈtʌtʃ wɪð/
global /ˈgləʊbl/
handkerchief /ˈhæŋkətʃɪf, -tʃiːf/
harbour /ˈhɑːbə(r)/
headphones /ˈhedfəʊnz/
illness /ˈɪlnəs/
immune /ɪˈmjuːn/
to infect /tu ɪnˈfekt/
influenza /ˌɪnfluˈenzə/
to be into /tə ˌbi ˈɪntə/
to mind your own business /tə ˌmaɪnd jɔːr ˌəʊn ˈbɪznəs/
MP3 player /ˌem ˌpiː ˈθriː ˌpleɪə(r)/
outbreak /ˈaʊtbreɪk/
pain /peɪn/
palmtop /ˈpɑːmtɒp/
pandemic /pænˈdemɪk/
pity /ˈpɪti/
possession /pəˈzeʃn/
questionnaire /ˌkwestʃəˈneə(r)/
saxophone /ˈsæksəfəʊn/
shot /ʃɒt/
since /sɪns/
sneeze /sniːz/
soul /səʊl/
spike /spaɪk/
spread /spred/
to be starving /tə ˌbi ˈstɑːvɪŋ/
to sulk /tə ˈsʌlk/
to take back /tə ˌteɪk ˈbæk/
tiny /ˈtaɪni/
troubled /ˈtrʌbld/
understanding /ˌʌndəˈstændɪŋ/

Unit 2

adventure /ədˈventʃə(r)/
advertisement /ədˈvɜːtɪsmənt/
afraid /əˈfreɪd/
agreement /əˈgriːmənt/
amateur /ˈæmətə(r)/
amazed /əˈmeɪzd/
animated /ˈænɪmeɪtɪd/
archaeologist /ˌɑːkiˈɒlədʒɪst/
article /ˈɑːtɪkl/
automated /ˈɔːtəmeɪtɪd/
blood /blʌd/
breakdown /ˈbreɪkdaʊn/
buggy /ˈbʌgi/
businessman /ˈbɪznəsmən/
buzz /bʌz/
canteen /kænˈtiːn/
to commit /tə kəˈmɪt/
cooperation /kəʊˌɒpəˈreɪʃn/
cover /ˈkʌvə(r)/
cosmetics /kɒzˈmetɪks/
crane /kreɪn/
creative /kriˈeɪtɪv/
crime /kraɪm/
currency /ˈkʌrənsi/
defence /dɪˈfens/
diameter /daɪˈæmətə(r)/
diet /ˈdaɪət/
dinosaur /ˈdaɪnəsɔː(r)/
economics /ˌiːkəˈnɒmɪks/
electric /ɪˈlektrɪk/
epic /ˈepɪk/
evil /ˈiːvl/
fantasy /ˈfæntəsi/
fence /fens/
gun /gʌn/
illegal /ɪˈliːgl/
ingredient /ɪnˈgriːdiənt/
international /ˌɪntəˈnæʃnəl/
just /dʒʌst, dʒəs(t)/
justice /ˈdʒʌstɪs/
kill /kɪl/
label /ˈleɪbl/
mechanic /məˈkænɪk/
movie /ˈmuːvi/
mosquito /məˈskiːtəʊ/
nightmare /ˈnaɪtmeə(r)/
parallel /ˈpærəlel/
peach /piːtʃ/
poker /ˈpəʊkə(r)/
police force /pəˈliːs ˌfɔːs/
popcorn /ˈpɒpkɔːn/
population /ˌpɒpjəˈleɪʃn/
prehistoric /ˌpriːhɪˈstɒrɪk/
prize /praɪz/
producer /prəˈdjuːsə(r)/
recent /ˈriːsnt/
regulation /ˌregjuˈleɪʃn/
resin /ˈrezɪn/
resort /rɪˈzɔːt/
responsible /rɪˈspɒnsəbl/
review /rɪˈvjuː/
scientist /ˈsaɪəntɪst/
sign /saɪn/
special effects /ˌspeʃl ɪˈfekts/
spymaster /ˈspaɪˌmɑːstə(r)/
stunt /stʌnt/
successful /səkˈsesfl/
terror /ˈterə(r)/
toiletries /ˈtɔɪlətriz/
toy /tɔɪ/
trap /træp/
treaty /ˈtriːti/
twice /twaɪs/
unusual /ʌnˈjuːʒuəl/
various /ˈveəriəs/
villain /ˈvɪlən/
violence /ˈvaɪələns/
violent /ˈvaɪələnt/
war /wɔː(r)/
yet /jet/

Unit 3

cache /kæʃ/
to carve out /tə ˌkɑːv ˈaʊt/
carving /ˈkɑːvɪŋ/
century /ˈsentʃəri/
coin /kɔɪn/
compressed /kəmˈprest/
continent /ˈkɒntɪnənt/
coordinates /kəʊˈɔːdɪnəts/
couple /ˈkʌpl/
to discover /tə dɪˈskʌvə(r)/
earrings /ˈɪərɪŋz/
exactly /ɪgˈzæktli/
field /fiːld/
flood /flʌd/
to flow /tə ˈfləʊ/
fresh water /ˌfreʃ ˈwɔːtə(r)/
geocaching /ˌdʒiːəʊˈkæʃɪŋ/
glacier /ˈglæsiə(r)/
GPS unit /ˌdʒiː ˌpiː ˈes ˌjuːnɪt/
ground /graʊnd/
handful /ˈhændfl/
to hide /tə ˈhaɪd/
to hunt /tə ˈhʌnt/
hydroelectric /ˌhaɪdrəʊɪˈlektrɪk/
to keep /tə ˈkiːp/
landscape /ˈlændskeɪp/
leader /ˈliːdə(r)/
mass /mæs/
to melt /tə ˈmelt/
moon /muːn/
motorway /ˈməʊtəweɪ/
mummy /ˈmʌmi/
ocean /ˈəʊʃn/
power /ˈpaʊə(r)/
production /prəˈdʌkʃn/
proud /praʊd/
to provide /tə prəˈvaɪd/
resources /rɪˈzɔːsɪz/
to rise /tə ˈraɪz/
sensation /senˈseɪʃn/
to shrink /tə ˈʃrɪŋk/
to sign up /tə ˌsaɪn ˈʌp/
stone /stəʊn/
to switch on /tə ˌswɪtʃ ˈɒn/
thick /θɪk/
treasure /ˈtreʒə(r)/
to water /tə ˈwɔːtə(r)/
waterfall /ˈwɔːtəfɔːl/
weight /weɪt/
worried /ˈwʌrid/

Unit 4

abroad /əˈbrɔːd/
ancient /ˈeɪnʃənt/
apologise /əˈpɒlədʒaɪz/
author /ˈɔːθə(r)/
to behave /tə bɪˈheɪv/
bestselling /bestˈselɪŋ/
to bump into /tə ˌbʌmp ˈɪntə/
character /ˈkærəktə(r)/
to come across /tə ˌkʌm əˈkrɒs/
to decide /tə dɪˈsaɪd/
depressed /dɪˈprest/
determined /dɪˈtɜːmɪnd/
dirt /dɜːt/
disappointed /ˌdɪsəˈpɔɪntɪd/
doorbell /ˈdɔːbel/
dynamic /daɪˈnæmɪk/
energetic /ˌenəˈdʒetɪk/
event /ɪˈvent/
extract /ˈekstrækt/
to fail /tə ˈfeɪl/
festival /ˈfestɪvl/
flexible /ˈfleksəbl/
foreign /ˈfɒrən/
to give up /tə ˌgɪv ˈʌp/
headmaster /hedˈmɑːstə(r)/

helpful /'helpfl/
intelligent /ɪn'telɪʤənt/
to invent /tu ɪn'vent/
to investigate /tu ɪn'vestɪgeɪt/
to justify /tə 'ʤʌstɪfaɪ/
lentil /'lentl/
location /ləʊ'keɪʃn/
to look into /tə ˌlʊk 'ɪntə/
lucky charm /ˌlʌki 'ʧɑ:m/
magpie /'mægpaɪ/
to make up /tə ˌmeɪk 'ʌp/
mark /mɑ:k/
mirror /'mɪrə(r)/
mixture /'mɪksʧə(r)/
multiple choice /ˌmʌltɪpl 'ʧɔɪs/
passionate /'pæʃənət/
pavement /'peɪvmənt/
positive /'pɒzətɪv/
to postpone /tə pəʊst'pəʊn/
proof /pru:f/
to put off /tə ˌpʊt 'ɒf/
result /rɪ'zʌlt/
to revise /tə rɪ'vaɪz/
rude /ru:d/
sense /sens/
to shine /tə 'ʃaɪn/
similar /'sɪmələ(r)/
to solve /tə 'sɒlv/
storyline /'stɔ:rilaɪn/
superstition /ˌsu:pə'stɪʃn/
superstitious /ˌsu:pə'stɪʃəs/
to sweep /tə 'swi:p/
symbol /'sɪmbl/
to take after /tə 'teɪk ˌɑ:ftə(r)/
trance /trɑ:ns/
to turn down /tə ˌtɜ:n 'daʊn/
to turn on /tə ˌtɜ:n 'ɒn/
typical /'tɪpɪkl/
web /web/
whisper /'wɪspə(r)/
wish /wɪʃ/
wonderful /'wʌndəfl/

Unit 5

aquarium /ə'kweəriəm/
architect /'ɑ:kɪtekt/
to arrest /tu ə'rest/
art gallery /'ɑ:t ˌgæləri/
assignment /ə'saɪnmənt/
atlas /'ætləs/
bagel /'beɪgl/
baker /'beɪkə(r)/
battle /'bætl/
beheaded /bɪ'hedɪd/
to bet /tə 'bet/
to blow up /tə ˌbləʊ 'ʌp/
bone /bəʊn/
brick /brɪk/
to burn down /tə ˌbɜ:n 'daʊn/
chilly /'ʧɪli/
column /'kɒləm/
completely /kəm'pli:tli/
concert /'kɒnsət/
cream cheese /ˌkri:m 'ʧi:z/
deer /dɪə(r)/
to defeat /tə dɪ'fi:t/
to design /tə dɪ'zaɪn/
to die /tə 'daɪ/
dockyards /'dɒkjɑ:dz/
exhibition /ˌeksɪ'bɪʃn/
factory /'fæktəri/
fly /flaɪ/
to gaze /tə 'geɪz/
to grow /tə 'grəʊ/
identification /aɪˌdentɪfɪ'keɪʃn/
intonation /ˌɪntə'neɪʃn/
to invade /tu ɪn'veɪd/
lazy /'leɪzi/
lousy /'laʊzi/
magnifying glass /'mægnɪfaɪɪŋ ˌglɑ:s/
market /'mɑ:kɪt/
marsh /mɑ:ʃ/
meaning /'mi:nɪŋ/
megastore /'megə ˌstɔ:(r)/
monarchy /'mɒnəki/
monument /'mɒnjəmənt/
narrow /'nærəʊ/
nurse /nɜ:s/
paradise /'pærədaɪs/
performance /pə'fɔ:məns/
pilot /'paɪlət/
port /pɔ:t/
programmer /'prəʊgræmə(r)/
reduction /rɪ'dʌkʃn/
republic /rɪ'pʌblɪk/
to rule /tə 'ru:l/
to sell out /tə ˌsel 'aʊt/
settlement /'setlmənt/
sheepdog /'ʃi:pdɒg/
to swarm /tə 'swɔ:m/
theatre /'θɪətə(r)/
to throw /tə 'θrəʊ/
tower /'taʊə(r)/
traffic warden /'træfɪk ˌwɔ:dn/
trailer /'treɪlə(r)/
tribe /traɪb/
to wander /tə 'wɒndə(r)/
weak /wi:k/
wood /wʊd/
wooden /'wʊdn/
writer /'raɪtə(r)/

Unit 6

advantage /əd'vɑ:ntɪʤ/
to allow /tu ə'laʊ/
apartheid /ə'pɑ:taɪt/
baseball /'beɪsbɔ:l/
border /'bɔ:də(r)/
to break out /tə ˌbreɪk 'aʊt/
cassette player /kə'set ˌpleɪə(r)/
cigarette /sɪgə'ret/
to clear away /tə ˌklɪər ə'weɪ/
cocoa bean /'kəʊkəʊ ˌbi:n/
community /kə'mju:nəti/
competition /ˌkɒmpə'tɪʃn/
disco /'dɪskəʊ/
to dye /tə 'daɪ/
electrician /ɪlek'trɪʃn/
to end up /tu ˌend 'ʌp/
grizzly bear /ˌgrɪzli 'beə(r)/
grown-up /ˌgrəʊn 'ʌp/
helmet /'helmɪt/
to hibernate /tə 'haɪbəneɪt/
housework /'haʊswɜ:k/
igloo /'ɪglu:/
immigrant /'ɪmɪgrənt/
independent /ˌɪndɪ'pendənt/
insect /'ɪnsekt/
lama /'lɑ:mə/
let /let/
loads /ləʊdz/
native speaker /ˌneɪtɪv 'spi:kə(r)/
olive oil /ˌɒlɪv 'ɔɪl/
parade /pə'reɪd/
peaceful /'pi:sfl/
to pronounce /tə prə'naʊns/
refugee /ˌrefju'ʤi:/
rhino /'raɪnəʊ/
salary /'sæləri/
seat /si:t/
to share /tə 'ʃeə(r)/
to smoke /tə 'sməʊk/
snow mobile /'snəʊ məˌbi:l/
tiring /'taɪərɪŋ/
truffle /'trʌfl/
volume /'vɒlju:m/
war-torn /'wɔ: ˌtɔ:n/

Unit 7

album /'ælbəm/
bamboo /bæm'bu:/
binding /'baɪndɪŋ/
blues /blu:z/
career /kə'rɪə(r)/
clarinet /klærɪ'net/
classical /'klæsɪkl/
compilation /ˌkɒmpɪ'leɪʃn/
complaint /kəm'pleɪnt/
country /'kʌntri/
crazy /'kreɪzi/
to demonstrate /tə 'demənstreɪt/
drummer /'drʌmə(r)/
folk /fəʊk/
gently /'ʤentli/
heavy metal /ˌhevi 'metl/
hip-hop /'hɪp ˌhɒp/
idol /'aɪdl/
indie /'ɪndi/
jazz /ʤæz/
lonely /'ləʊnli/
to be made up of /tə ˌbi 'meɪd ˌʌp əv/
massive /'mæsɪv/
metallic /mə'tælɪk/
musician /mju:'zɪʃn/
neighbour /'neɪbə(r)/
neither /'naɪðə(r)/
noise /nɔɪz/
opening /'əʊpnɪŋ/
out of tune /ˌaʊt əv 'tju:n/
punk /pʌŋk/
rap /ræp/
to remind /tə rɪ'maɪnd/
roof /ru:f/
to scream /tə 'skri:m/
set /set/
to shoot /tə 'ʃu:t/
so /səʊ/
stage /steɪʤ/
stuff /stʌf/
talent show /'tælənt ˌʃəʊ/
training /'treɪnɪŋ/
tube /tju:b/
TV series /ˌti: 'vi: ˌsɪəri:z/
vocals /'vəʊklz/

Unit 8

to affect /tu ə'fekt/
aftershock /'ɑ:ftəʃɒk/
to amuse /tu ə'mju:z/
approximately /ə'prɒksɪmətli/
artist /'ɑ:tɪst/
ash /æʃ/
ashore /ə'ʃɔ:(r)/
avalanche /'ævəlɑ:nʃ/
berry /'beri/
caption /'kæpʃn/
castaway /'kɑ:stəweɪ/
catastrophe /kə'tæstrəfi/
coconut /'kəʊkənʌt/
to collapse /tə kə'læps/
comic /'kɒmɪk/
to control /tə kən'trəʊl/
to crush /tə 'krʌʃ/
desert island /ˌdezət 'aɪlənd/
disaster /dɪ'zɑ:stə(r)/
dishwasher /'dɪʃwɒʃə(r)/
drought /draʊt/
dynamite /'daɪnəmaɪt/
earth /ɜ:θ/
earthquake /'ɜ:θkweɪk/
to erupt /tu ɪ'rʌpt/
to escape /tu ɪ'skeɪp/

to evacuate /tu ɪ'vækjueɪt/
explosion /ɪk'spləʊʒn/
flare /fleə(r)/
fox /fɒks/
hurricane /'hʌrikən/
lava /'lɑ:və/
light bulb /'laɪt ˌbʌlb/
literature /'lɪtrətʃə(r)/
local /'ləʊkl/
make-believe /'meɪk bɪˌli:v/
miracle /'mɪrəkl/
mud /mʌd/
mudslide /'mʌdslaɪd/
nuclear reactor /ˌnju:kliə ri'æktə(r)/
package /'pækɪʤ/
to panic /tə 'pænɪk/
peers /pɪəz/
to protect /tə prə'tekt/
raft /rɑ:ft/
to reach /tə 'ri:ʧ/
to run into /tə ˌrʌn 'ɪntə/
to rush /tə 'rʌʃ/
scale /skeɪl/
to serve /tə 'sɜ:v/
to shake /tə 'ʃeɪk/
to slide /tə 'slaɪd/
society /sə'saɪəti/
strength /streŋθ/
suitcase /'su:tkeɪs/
survival /sə'vaɪvl/
to survive /tə sə'vaɪv/
sympathy /'sɪmpəθi/
telephone /'telɪfəʊn/
temple /'templ/
tremor /'tremə(r)/
tsunami /tsu:'nɑ:mi/
volcano /vɒl'keɪnəʊ/
warning /'wɔ:nɪŋ/
webpage /'webpeɪʤ/
website /'websaɪt/
windscreen wipers /'wɪndskri:n ˌwaɪpəz/

Unit 9

to add /tu 'æd/
alibi /'ælɪbaɪ/
babysitting /'beɪbisɪtɪŋ/
bill /bɪl/
bowl /bəʊl/
built-in /ˌbɪlt 'ɪn/
to charge /tə 'ʧɑ:ʤ/
CD-ROM /ˌsi: ˌdi: 'rɒm/
circular /'sɜ:kjələ(r)/
clockwise /'klɒkwaɪz/
coach /kəʊʧ/
cup final /'kʌp ˌfaɪnl/
definitely /'defɪnətli/
desktop /'desktɒp/
diagonal /daɪ'ægənl/
digit /'dɪʤɪt/
dilemma /daɪ'lemə/
door key /'dɔ: ki:/
doubt /daʊt/
to earn /tu 'ɜ:n/
to fold /tə 'fəʊld/
grade /greɪd/
half /hɑ:f/
horizontal /ˌhɒrɪ'zɒntl/
keyboard /'ki:bɔ:d/
LAN /læn/
to lead to /tə 'li:d tə/
modem /'məʊdem/
to multiply /tə 'mʌltɪplaɪ/
notebook /'nəʊtbʊk/
opinion /ə'pɪnjən/
paper round /'peɪpə ˌraʊnd/
printer /'prɪntə(r)/
relationship /rɪ'leɪʃnʃɪp/
repair /rɪ'peə(r)/
ridiculous /rɪ'dɪkjələs/
to seal /tə 'si:l/
speakers /'spi:kəz/
specialist /'speʃəlɪst/
strict /strɪkt/
to subtract /tə səb'trækt/
sum /sʌm/
total /'təʊtl/
USB stick /ˌju: ˌes 'bi: ˌstɪk/
vet /vet/

Unit 10

aim /eɪm/
background /'bækgraʊnd/
balcony /'bælkəni/
bear /beə(r)/
delta /'deltə/
den /den/
dimwit /'dɪmwɪt/
envious /'enviəs/
equipment /ɪ'kwɪpmənt/
expedition /ˌekspə'dɪʃn/
flight /flaɪt/
gap year /'gæp ˌjɪə(r)/
in case /ˌɪn 'keɪs/
ink /ɪŋk/
to be kidding /tə ˌbi 'kɪdɪŋ/
leadership /'li:dəʃɪp/
leopard /'lepəd/
must /mʌst, məs(t)/
opportunity /ˌɒpə'tju:nəti/
park ranger /ˌpɑ:k 'reɪnʤə(r)/
permanent /'pɜ:mənənt/
to plot /tə 'plɒt/
to protest /tə prə'test/
route /ru:t/
safari /sə'fɑ:ri/
self-confidence /ˌself 'kɒnfɪdəns/
skill /skɪl/
spot /spɒt/
volunteer /ˌvɒlən'tɪə(r)/
wetland /'wetlənd/
wilderness /'wɪldənəs/
windsurfing /'wɪndsɜ:fɪŋ/

Unit 11

to admire /tu əd'maɪə(r)/
alternative /ɔ:l'tɜ:nətɪv/
appliance /ə'plaɪəns/
average /'ævərɪʤ/
blackout /'blækaʊt/
blank /blæŋk/
bottle /'bɒtl/
consumption /kən'sʌmpʃn/
container /kən'teɪnə(r)/
controversial /ˌkɒntrə'vɜ:ʃl/
council /'kaʊnsl/
current /'kʌrənt/
democracy /dɪ'mɒkrəsi/
ecology /ɪ'kɒləʤi/
economy /ɪ'kɒnəmi/
eco-warrior /'i:kəʊ ˌwɒriə(r)/
energy /'enəʤi/
entrance /'entrəns/
to face /tə 'feɪs/
to found /tə 'faʊnd/
French fries /ˌfrenʧ 'fraɪz/
heat /hi:t/
hero /'hɪərəʊ/
heroine /'herəʊɪn/
increase /'ɪŋkri:s/
insulation /ˌɪnsju'leɪʃn/
law /lɔ:/
lawyer /'lɔ:jə(r)/
leaflet /'li:flət/
litter lout /'lɪtə ˌlaʊt/
march /mɑ:ʧ/
marine /mə'ri:n/
to marry /tə 'mæri/
to object /tu əb'ʤekt/
to overcome /tu ˌəʊvə'kʌm/
parliament /'pɑ:ləmənt/
petition /pə'tɪʃn/
petrol pump /'petrəl ˌpʌmp/
planner /'plænə(r)/
plan of action /ˌplæn əv 'ækʃn/
to plant /tə 'plɑ:nt/
playing field /'pleɪɪŋ ˌfi:ld/
poison /'pɔɪzn/
pond /pɒnd/
to power /tə 'paʊə(r)/
protest /'prəʊtest/
to recycle /tə ˌri:'saɪkl/
to refuse /tə rɪ'fju:z/
to remove /tə rɪ'mu:v/
renewable energy /rɪˌnju:əbl 'enəʤi/
rights /raɪts/
seriously /'sɪəriəsli/
single mother /ˌsɪŋgl 'mʌðə(r)/
slogan /'sləʊgən/
solar panel /ˌsəʊlə 'pænl/
source /sɔ:s/
to stand up for /tə ˌstænd 'ʌp fə/
stove /stəʊv/
straightaway /ˌstreɪtə'weɪ/
to support /tə sə'pɔ:t/
tennis court /'tenɪs ˌkɔ:t/
tide /taɪd/
traditional /trə'dɪʃənl/
treehouse /'tri:haʊs/
tunnel /'tʌnl/
washing machine /'wɒʃɪŋ məˌʃi:n/
wind turbine /'wɪnd ˌtɜ:baɪn/

Unit 12

to afford /tu ə'fɔ:d/
blond /blɒnd/
casual /'kæʒuəl/
charts /ʧɑ:ts/
contrast /'kɒntrɑ:st/
copper /'kɒpə(r)/
deal /di:l/
diverse /daɪ'vɜ:s/
easy-listening /ˌi:zi 'lɪsnɪŋ/
elegant /'elɪgənt/
to experience /tu ɪk'spɪəriəns/
film studio /'fɪlm ˌstju:diəʊ/
generation /ˌʤenə'reɪʃn/
to hand out /tə ˌhænd 'aʊt/
hand-print /'hændprɪnt/
handset /'hændset/
to identify /tu aɪ'dentɪfaɪ/
incredible /ɪn'kredəbl/
influential /ˌɪnflu'enʃl/
lie /laɪ/
material /mə'tɪəriəl/
muscular /'mʌskjələ(r)/
national park /ˌnæʃnəl 'pɑ:k/
pipe /paɪp/
politician /ˌpɒlə'tɪʃn/
to release /tə rɪ'li:s/
to reuse /tə ˌri:'ju:z/
rubbish tip /'rʌbɪʃ ˌtɪp/
scheme /ski:m/
scruffy /'skrʌfi/
to separate /tə 'sepəreɪt/
smart /smɑ:t/
sophisticated /sə'fɪstɪkeɪtɪd/
sporty /'spɔ:ti/
strip /strɪp/
torn /tɔ:n/
traffic cone /'træfɪk ˌkəʊn/
up-and-coming /ˌʌp ən 'kʌmɪŋ/
waste /weɪst/
well-built /ˌwel 'bɪlt/

Pronunciation guide

Vowels

/iː/	see
/ɪ/	bit
/e/	bed
/æ/	sad
/ɑː/	father
/ʌ/	cut
/ʊ/	cook
/uː/	too
/i/	happy
/ə/	above
/ɒ/	got
/ɔː/	saw
/u/	actual

Diphthongs

/ɜː/	circle
/eɪ/	say
/aɪ/	buy
/ɔɪ/	boy
/əʊ/	go
/aʊ/	now
/ɪə/	hear
/eə/	hair
/ʊə/	sure
/juː/	few
/aɪə/	fire
/aʊə/	power

Consonants

/p/	push
/b/	bank
/t/	time
/d/	diary
/k/	carpet
/g/	big
/f/	surf
/v/	very
/θ/	thin
/ð/	that
/s/	sit
/z/	zero
/ʃ/	shine
/ʒ/	measure
/h/	hot
/w/	water
/tʃ/	chair
/dʒ/	joke
/m/	more
/n/	snow
/ŋ/	sing
/r/	ring
/l/	small
/j/	you

CAMBRIDGE UNIVERSITY PRESS
www.cambridge.org/elt

HELBLING LANGUAGES
www.helblinglanguages.com

More! 3 Student's Book
by Herbert Puchta & Jeff Stranks
with G. Gerngross C. Holzmann P. Lewis-Jones

First Published 2008
4th printing 2010

Printed in Dubai by Oriental Press

A catalogue record for this publication is available from the British Library

ISBN 978-0-521-71307-8 More! 3 Student's Book with interactive CD-ROM (Windows)
ISBN 978-0-521-71308-5 More! 3 Workbook with CD (audio)
ISBN 978-0-521-71309-2 More! 3 Teacher's Book
ISBN 978-0-521-71310-8 More! 3 Teacher's Resource Pack with Testbuilder CD-ROM (Windows)/CD (audio)
ISBN 978-0-521-71311-5 More! 3 Class CDs (audio)
ISBN 978-0-521-71312-2 More! 3 Extra Practice Book
ISBN 978-0-521-71313-9 More! 3 DVD (PAL/NTSC)

The authors would like to thank those people who have made significant contributions towards the final form of MORE! INTERNATIONAL:

Oonagh Wade and Rosamund Cantalamessa for their expertise in working on the manuscripts, their useful suggestions for improvement, and the support we got from them.

Lucia Astuti and Markus Spielmann, Helbling Languages, Ron Ragsdale and James Dingle, Cambridge University Press, for their dedication to the project and innovative publishing vision.

Our designers, Amanda Hockin, Greg Sweetnam, Quantico, Craig Cornell and Niels Gyde for their imaginative layouts and stimulating creativity. Also, our artwork assistants, Silvia Scorzoso and Francesca Gironi, for their dedicated work.

The publisher would like to thank the following for their kind permission to riproduce the following photograph and other copyright material:

Alamy p6, p13, p14, p23, p26, p31, 33 (Tuvalu), p34, p45, p46, p49, p50, p54, p56, p58, p65, p66, p69, p70, p71, p72 (bouzouki; folk band), p74, p76, p82, p83, p95, p102, p109, p110, p111, p113 (turbine), p114, p115, p119, p122, p123; **Corbis** p69 (Beatles performing in Germany), p123 (Red Hot Chilli Peppers); **Dkimages** p32, p52, p53; **Gary Braasch** p33 (Pasterze Glacier); **Getty Images** p15; **Günter Gerngross** p99; **Helbling Languages** p86 (modem; notebook; printer; USB stick); **Herbert Puchta** p113 (petrol station); **©iStockphoto.com**/prominx (sunglasses) p6 /PhotoEuphoria p12 /qingwa p30 /thinair28 p31 / jsmith p56 (doctor) /ZlatKOstic / dinna79 /Rouzes p86 (DVD-R/W; speakers; flat screen) /Gelpi p120; **Shutterstock** Elnur (headphones) p6, Sebastian Kaulitzki p13, Eduard Härkönen, Brandon Seidel p22, Suzanne Tucker, Jason Stitt p25, PhotoSky 4t com p31 (walking), vospalej p50 (Cindy), David Hughes p53 (The Globe theatre today), Supri Suharjoto (computer programmer), TebNad, PhotoSky 4t com p59, M.E. Mulder, Blaz Kure p72 (sitar; Andean flute), Alex Melnick, Tomasz Gulla, Albo, ilker canikligil p86, Olga Semicheva p93, Ioannis Ioannou p112, egd, V. J. Matthew, irabel8, Ilja Mašík p113, Mikhail Nekrasov p115 (Cairo); **Wikimedia Commons** p22 (Mercosur), Sönke Kraft (mijwiz).

The publishers would like to thank the following illustrators:

Roberto Battestini; Moreno Chiacchiera; Michele Farella; Pierluigi Longo; Gastone Mencherini.

The publishers would like to thank the following for their assistance with commissioned photographs:

David Tolley Ltd. pp 4, 14, 24, 34, 54, 64, 74, 76, 84, 104, 114.